Finding God

Beyond Religion

A Guide for Skeptics,
Agnostics & Unorthodox Believers
Inside & Outside the Church

TOM STELLA

Foreword by The Rev. Canon Marianne Wells Borg

Walking Together, Finding the Way®

SKYLIGHT PATHS®
PUBLISHING
Woodstock, Vermont

Finding God Beyond Religion:
A Guide for Skeptics, Agnostics & Unorthodox Believers Inside & Outside the Church

2013 Quality Paperback Edition, First Printing
© 2013 by Tom Stella
Foreword © 2013 by Marianne Wells Borg

For information regarding permission to reprint material from this book, please mail or fax your request in writing to SkyLight Paths Publishing, Permissions Department, at the address / fax number listed below, or e-mail your request to permissions@ skylightpaths.com

Grateful acknowledgment is given for permission to use material from the following source: p.xi, "The Place Where We Are Right" by Yehuda Amichai, in *The Selected Poetry of Yehuda Amichai*, edited and translated by Chana Bloch and Stephen Mitchell. © 1996 by Chana Bloch and Stephen Mitchell. Republished by permission of the University of California Press.

Library of Congress Cataloging-in-Publication Data

Stella, Tom.
  Finding God beyond religion : a guide for skeptics, agnostics & unorthodox believers inside & outside the church / Tom Stella. —2013 quality paperback edition.
     pages cm
  Includes bibliographical references (pages 121–124).
  ISBN 978-1-59473-485-4
1. Spiritual life—Christianity. I. Title.
  BV4501.3.S738 2013
  248.4—dc23

                              2013002736

10 9 8 7 6 5 4 3 2 1

Manufactured in the United States of America
Cover Design: Jenny Buono
Interior Design: Kelley Barton

SkyLight Paths Publishing is creating a place where people of different spiritual traditions come together for challenge and inspiration, a place where we can help each other understand the mystery that lies at the heart of our existence.

SkyLight Paths sees both believers and seekers as a community that increasingly transcends traditional boundaries of religion and denomination—people wanting to learn from each other, *walking together, finding the way.*

SkyLight Paths, "Walking Together, Finding the Way," and colophon are trademarks of LongHill Partners, Inc., registered in the U.S. Patent and Trademark Office.

Walking Together, Finding the Way®
Published by SkyLight Paths Publishing
A Division of LongHill Partners, Inc.
Sunset Farm Offices, Route 4, P.O. Box 237
Woodstock, VT 05091
Tel: (802) 457-4000   Fax: (802) 457-4004
www.skylightpaths.com

Also by Tom Stella

The God Instinct:
Heeding Your Heart's Unrest

A Faith Worth Believing:
Finding New Life Beyond the Rules of Religion

It is with immense gratitude that I dedicate this book to my mother, Pearl Stella. Despite having lost both parents by the age of five, she has mastered the art of motherhood—Italian style! The totality with which she has given herself to her family and the hands-on nature of her love for her children has given my siblings and me a glimpse into the unconditional, incarnate love that is God. Her work ethic, even now at ninety-three, is a source of inspiration. Her mastery of the arts of cooking and gardening have nourished the bodies of all who have feasted at her table and the souls of those who have gazed upon her yard. Her down-to-earth spirituality is the embodiment of all I attempt to convey in these pages. *Gratia Bella.*

Everybody has a double duty in life, to maintain a cultural life and a religious life.... So many religious institutions today focus on the cultural life almost exclusively instead of helping people cultivate a different kind of consciousness.

—Robert Johnson, *Balancing Heaven and Earth*

The astonishing discovery of the Gnostic gospels—a cache of ancient secret gospels and other revelations attributed to Jesus and his disciples—has revealed a much wider range of Christian groups than we had ever known before.... Many of these Christians saw themselves as not so much believers as seekers, people who "seek for God."

—Elaine Pagels, *Beyond Belief*

Logos—reason, the belief in obligatory doctrine as the word of God—has replaced *mythos* ... the belief that God cannot be known but that the enduring effort to find God is the essence of spirituality.

—Karen Armstrong

Every religion has a mystical core. The challenge is to find access to it and to live in its power.

—David Steindl-Rast

Contents

Foreword

From the place where we are right
Flowers will never grow
In the spring.
The place where we are right
Is hard and trampled
Like a yard.
But doubts and loves
Dig up the world
Like a mole, a plow.
And a whisper will be heard in the place
Where the ruined
House once stood.

                              —Yehuda Amichai

Doubts and loves. Doubts and loves move us to seek, to explore; they compel us to risk the possibility of "the More"—a term psychologist and philosopher William James used to refer to the Sacred. Tom Stella has been moved, shaped, liberated by doubts and loves. And through his doubts and loves, because of his doubts and loves, he has encountered and continues to encounter "the More." He encourages us to allow our own doubts and loves to call the questions as we search for God and what it means to be Christian in this twenty-first century.

The timing for this book couldn't be better. The conditions and state of our current religious and cultural world demand that we reexamine our claims, our hopes, our nature, our responsibilities as human beings. It is time for a new *aggiornamento*, a "bringing up to date" for the church and for seekers of God. Tom's book is such an *aggiornamento*. He explores prayer, belief, Jesus, the Bible, morality, the problem of evil, and the mission of the church with tenderness of heart, keen intellect, care, clarity, and disarming simplicity. In so doing, he gives us permission to examine afresh our own encounters with conventional faith, litmus statements of belief, and the norms they espouse. At the end of each chapter, he provides further questions for our continued reflection. They are worthy of our time and to take into conversation with others.

I would like to underscore a theme that is the *basso continuo* of this book as well as the theological jewel at its center: the power, reality, mystery of the incarnation. Throughout this book Tom gives witness to the holiness that resides in each of us, for God comes "in the flesh." God is with us and God is within us. But "God is not just within us," Tom insists, "God *is* the within of us." This is our deepest and original imprint. Once we perceive this reality in ourselves and in others, it changes everything. And we will come to see doubts and loves like prisms reflecting all manner of light and shadow. Darkness as well as light is all part of the shimmering reality of our sacredness. Tom calls us to embrace ourselves as we are embraced.

Tom has put his hand to the plow, disturbed his own tightly compacted path, and in the process unsettled the very ground upon which he walks to find the Ground of being. He invites us to share in this "spiritual path ... the hilarious term" and he quotes Annie Dillard, "for those night-blind mesas and flayed hills on which people grope, for decades on end, with the goal of knowing the absolute." Tom's book is a light unto such paths, a steadying staff for such uncertain terrain. Tom Stella is himself a sure and trustworthy guide in our search for God and, if our search requires it, finding God *beyond* religion.

Let the words of this book and the life that it reflects companion you as you seek a deeper communion with the one who has called you and will sustain you. Great courage and humility will be required on the journey you undertake, and what will be revealed is the numinous nature of your ordinary and remarkable life. You are in good hands.

I write this on the last Sunday of the season of the Epiphany, the last Sunday before Lent. I write in liminal time, a transitional time, time poised at the initial stage of a process. Tom suggests we are all living in liminal time, "a transitional time between an epoch of religion that is on the decline and an epoch of spirituality that is on the rise." A time when, on a personal scale and on a religious and cultural one, we are struggling with doubts and loves, living upon earth that holds seeds, earth that can be hard and trampled and has the capacity to make the desert bloom. We stand at a threshold. Do we see a "ruined house" or morning in a new land?

The Rev. Canon Marianne Wells Borg

Introduction

"Out beyond ideas of wrongdoing and right doing there is a field, I'll meet you there."[1] With these words, Muslim mystic and poet Jelaluddin Rumi (1207–1273) invites us to leave behind the narrow notion of religion understood as moral teachings and to enter the field where spiritual seekers gather.

The mythical place where Rumi encourages us to rendezvous with him is that field of dreams Taoists refer to as the "palace of nowhere where all the many things are one." Like most fields, it is a wide expanse; like many dreams, it is free of the confinement of convention and logic; and like a palace, it is majestic because it is home to the truth that life and death, sacred and secular, time and eternity, and Divinity and humanity are not disparate things but dimensions of one vast and sacred mystery.

This worldview is one that resonates with those whose longing for ultimate truth has not been satisfied by conventional religion. Many of us are uninspired by traditional worship and unmoved by teachings that tend to reinforce the notion that matters of faith are more about mastery than mystery, more defined than unconfined.

Despite their dissatisfaction with traditional religion, some people continue to linger in the vestibule of the church, keeping at least one foot in the building of their faith family. The need for fellowship, sacraments, and service are often fulfilled in the context of church communities; these can give meaning to church membership even when a deeper, more challenging interpretation of religious teachings is absent.

But many others, who no longer find it possible to straddle two worlds, are drawn to chart a course on what Pulitzer Prize–winning author Annie Dillard has called the "spiritual path":

> "Spiritual path" is the hilarious popular term for those night-blind mesas and flayed hills on which people grope, for decades on end, with the goal of knowing the absolute. They discover others spread under the stars and encamped here and there by watch fires, in groups or alone, in the open landscape; they stop for a sleep, or for several years, and move along without knowing toward what or why.[2]

Such a venture is not for the faint of heart. Because Dillard's "path" is fraught with uncertainty, it is precarious. Because "ideas of wrongdoing and right doing" can provide us with a sense of security and meaning in what appears to be life's randomness, it is no small undertaking to embark on the journey to which Rumi beckons us. Who would not prefer the warmth of home—that is, the security of a church with its familiar devotions and rituals and its predictable beliefs and teachings—to the unfamiliar and unpredictable "road less traveled"?

Embracing the Invitation to Uncertainty

What has become apparent to me in my work as a priest, hospital and hospice chaplain, spiritual director, and retreat facilitator is that life on the spiritual path is the preference of a growing number; there is a spiritual movement afoot. There is in our culture nothing less than an exodus from what many experience as religion resistant to renewal; that is, to churches that have so rigidly defined their teachings and traditions that they have ceased to adapt to the needs of those whose spiritual growth has led them to doubt, to question, or to believe differently about the tenets of their faith.

And so, on the march toward Rumi's field is that ragtag lot of skeptics, agnostics, and unorthodox believers who are searching not for security but for truth, not for the comfort provided by unexamined beliefs but for the faith that enables one to discover God even in the darkness of confusion and doubt.

Often, our spiritual journey either begins with, or brings us to, a crisis of faith. No longer sustained by easy answers, we may find ourselves standing before a three-pronged fork in the road: we can wander in the direction of conventional beliefs and practices, we can reject God and turn away from religion altogether, or we can embrace our uncertainty as an invitation to a more vital understanding of both God and religion.

I have stumbled along the paths of convention and rebellion for some time but have now chosen to walk the way of invitation. I have done so because I am convinced of the importance of religious institutions and because I believe it is possible to reinterpret their teachings in a manner that gives them new meaning and can give us a new perspective on life.

Personally, I experienced a sense of vitality when I realized that religion was not primarily a road map guiding us to God in heaven but that its purpose was to awaken us to the truth that, in the words of priest and poet Gerard Manley Hopkins, "the world is charged with the grandeur of God."[3] With that realization, I began looking at life with the freshness of a child's eyes. What had been routine now felt new. That which had ceased to engage me now did so. And those people to whom I had grown accustomed (myself included) now became a source of wonder.

This book is written in response to my having encountered God in the world. It is the product of my passion and is therefore a love letter of sorts, penned with the conviction that religion should be less about rules and more about a relationship with the Divine incarnate in nature and in our human nature.

The Spiritual Meaning of Religious Truths

In the pages that follow, I revisit nine traditional aspects of religion that I consider central to the Christian faith to help you understand them in new and more spiritually uplifting ways. I write both for those who have left the church and for those who try—often unsuccessfully—to deepen their spiritual lives within it. What I have written are not findings from the exhaustive research of a scholar, but conclusions that are the fruit of my own soul-searching attempt to discover new meaning in the timeless truths of the Christian tradition. I articulate these conclusions not only to help myself become clear about my beliefs, but also to fan the flame of faith that has begun to die in so many people I know and in the countless others who are like them.

I begin by examining views of God—why not start at the top? Many of those called to rendezvous with Rumi and accompany Dillard can no longer relate to the traditional understanding of God as a Supreme Being, a "guy in the sky," but are at a loss about to whom or to what the word *God* refers. Yet when we begin to view God as the spiritual essence at the heart of creation—what theologian Paul Tillich describes as "Ground of being"—not only God but life itself can take on new meaning, because this notion implies that we realize it is infused with divinity.

Central to our journey with and to God is the practice of prayer, which is the subject of chapter 2. Because their notion of God may have changed from one of a Supreme Being to Ground of being, many who consider themselves spiritual seekers find it difficult if not meaningless to pray as they once did; namely, to say prayers of praise, thanksgiving, and petition. But when our notion of God becomes more expansive, prayer becomes more a matter of communion than communication.

In chapter 3 I explore the meaning and misunderstandings of the terms *belief* and *faith*. Because the words *belief* and *faith* are often used synonymously, when we begin to question the foundational beliefs of our religious tradition it is assumed that our faith is weak. However, when faith is distinguished as a matter of entrusting ourselves to God, understood as one with life, we can have a strong faith (a willingness to let go and let God) even as we continue to wrestle with traditional religious teachings or no longer believe in them as we once did.

The founding fathers and mothers of every spiritual tradition run the risk of being seen as otherworldly or larger than life. Jesus, for Christians, has fallen prey to this fate. In chapter 4 we look at ways the Spirit can move us beyond the confines of conventional thinking about Jesus; for instance, that he was sent from above, born of a virgin, and that he died for our sins. When he is viewed from the perspective of "low Christology"— that is, understanding Jesus as a unique human—it becomes possible to both affirm his full humanity—any faults and idiosyncrasies included—and to recognize the divinity of our humanity.

When we realize that, in the words of Teilhard de Chardin, "We are spiritual beings having a human experience," the term *mystic* becomes one we can relate to. In chapter 5 we examine why *mystic*, which typically refers to one who lives with a felt sense of communion with God, is a term that applies to those of us who are more down-to-earth. Because institutional religious teachings often emphasize—or perhaps overemphasize— humankind's sinful nature, the notion that we are mystics can help us affirm our innate goodness.

Depending on our view of them, the sacred texts of all religions can be a force for good or a justification for inflicting harm. For Christians, the Bible has been both. When conventional Christian beliefs no longer resonate, a literal interpretation of the Bible ceases to make sense or to satisfy. In chapter 6 we examine how leaving literalism behind can help us recognize the metaphorical meaning of scripture, and the ageless, universal, and personal truth of its stories.

All religious traditions offer their followers teachings on morality, rules of behavior meant to steer us toward positive ways of relating to others. But morality easily morphs into moralism, a rigid overemphasis on sin and an afterlife motivation for our actions (fear of hell, hope for heaven). In chapter 7 I introduce the notion that when we begin to embrace God as benevolent, the focus of morality shifts to a right relationship, a living in harmony with the Spirit that is love, compassion, forgiveness, and the like.

Because God is generally thought to be both all-loving and all-powerful, the reality of evil has been a problem for many believers. Why, if God is so kind and capable, is evil so prevalent? In chapter 8 I propose that perhaps the problem of evil has to do with the commonly held assumption that God can or should prevent it. To posit that God is the Ground of being, wedded to life in good times and bad, affirms the possibility that God is present even in the midst of evil and injustice.

The book concludes with a consideration of the church that is a source of life for some, frustration for others, and both for many. When the church is experienced primarily as institutional, it ceases to nourish the soul. But as I show in chapter 9, when it remains true to its mission, when it enhances the spiritual well-being of its constituents, church and the community it creates can become an important factor in our search for wholeness and holiness.

In each chapter I share my personal experience and draw from the experience of others who also long to discover the spiritual meaning of religious truths. At the conclusion of each chapter, I provide "Questions for Your Own Journey" to help you navigate yours.

In Search of Food for the Soul

I consider it nothing less than a tragedy that so many intelligent, faith-filled, and spiritually grounded people do not find sustenance for their souls in worship services or in church-sponsored classes. Churches once filled with believers are now half-empty for many reasons, but the one most regrettable in my mind is that people hungry for what will feed and nourish their souls often find only the thin broth of religious righteousness and the pious party line. They are fed a theology that sustained them in their youth, when they were satisfied with meager meals consisting of biblical stories, understood literally, and moral directives designed, by the threat of punishment (hell) and the promise of reward (heaven), to make them pleasing to God. But they do not receive what their souls now crave: a hearty message that has the ability to strengthen and empower them for the responsibilities to which a mature faith and an adult life call them.

The growth of our bodies requires healthy, hearty food. The development of our souls requires spiritual nourishment capable of meeting the demands that come with maturity. Our understanding of religious truths can and should make us capable of living dynamic, productive, responsible, and meaningful lives. I hope the interpretation of the truths I offer here will get you started and that they will not only nourish your soul but also whet your appetite for more.

Bon appetit!

1

God Beyond Religion

Perhaps the greatest disaster of human history is one
that happened to or within religion: that is the con-
ceptual division between the holy and the world, the
excerpting of the Creator from creation.

—Wendell Berry, *A Continuous Harmony*

The author of this epigraph is not only a writer but a farmer
as well. Berry's books speak eloquently of the rural South,
life on the land, and the spirituality of creation. His earthy
understanding of the holiness of the simple life and of nature's
ways is based on the belief that God is not apart from creation
but one with it. For Berry, and for many who no longer find
meaning in the notion of God as a Supreme Being (theism), the
Divine is now considered the ground, the spiritual humus, the
nonmaterial and sacred stuff of which everything consists and
in which everything exists and grows.

The Judging God

I first learned about God within the confines of traditional religion. It was there, in church and catechism classes, that I was
given the message that "He" was someone somewhere else who
would, from time to time and in response to fervent prayer,

intervene on behalf of the righteous. The Holy and the world, the Creator and creation were not one but two.

This God is made in the image of humanity, with physical attributes usually thought to be male (complete with beard and booming voice); emotional attributes consisting of the extremes of love and anger, jealousy and mercy, and so on; and mental attributes usually considered to be a plan that must be discerned—God's will, or the "mind of God."

The God I encountered within religion was one who judged my every action and who made a judgment about the reward or punishment I would receive beyond this life. The notion of God as judge is present in the Bible, especially in the Hebrew Scriptures, where in Psalm 7:12 it states that God is a just judge who rebukes in anger every day. Mythologist Joseph Campbell claims that "people think of their God as having sentiments as we do, liking these people better than those, and having certain rules for their lives."[1] I grew up believing that God only loved those who always kept the rules of religion, not those who, like me, did so inconsistently.

I have experienced in myself and have witnessed in others the limiting, debilitating, and sometimes paralyzing effect of the belief in God thus understood. I know many people who no longer believe that God is distant and punitive but who continue to fear God. One of those people, Charles, told me about a dream he had in which his father said that if he continued to misbehave, he would surely fall into sin. Charles then spoke about how critical and nonaffirming his father had been toward him and his siblings when they were young, and that he now realized that he had projected this negativity onto God, whom he felt he could never please.

The notion of God as a critical parent packs a powerful emotional charge, the freedom from which is often a gradual, hard-won, and lifelong process. It has taken me years of study, countless meetings with spiritual directors, and many hours of prayer to begin embracing God as personal rather than as a person, as a part of life rather than apart from it, and as compassionate rather than punitive. Liberation from the oppressive effects of a negative theism is not easily attained. Achieving this freedom requires learning how not to cede power to guilt and how to embrace a faith that is based on the conviction that the true God may not be the God about whom many of us first learned.

Discovering a Different God

In contrast to this, the God of Rumi's field, Dillard's path, and Berry's farm is not found within religion, but beyond it; that is, beyond the doctrines and dogmas, the creeds and claims that speak of God as a being separate from creation. To discover God beyond religion is to uncover God in the midst of life. In our groping, we may stumble upon the Holy in nature as well as in church. We sometimes hear the Sacred sounding through popular songs as well as religious hymns. We may be guided by God's word in novels and poetry as well as in scripture. And our souls may be renewed by immersion in our hobbies as well as through participation in devotional practices.

Those who grope along the "night-blind mesas and flayed hills" that make up the spiritual path not only search for God beyond religion but do so, Dillard claims, "with the goal of knowing the absolute"; that is, in the hope of experiencing God in the frayed fabric of life itself. For those of us who wander this path, God is found not only in the heavens but in the midst of our lives: here, where we live and work; here, in us and in others, Divinity lurks omnipresent. This is not a New Age concept but one that is age-old, for scripture states: "In God we live and move and exist" (Acts 17:28).

The notion that God is present in the nitty-gritty of life is also found in Celtic spirituality, which is characterized by earthiness and speaks of "thin places" where the omnipresence of God is experienced in a very real, tangible way. The Irish poet, philosopher, and scholar John O'Donohue articulates the essence of Celtic spirituality when he writes:

> The Celtic mind was not burdened by dualism. It did not separate what belongs together.... The dualism that separates the visible from the invisible, time from eternity, the human from the divine, was totally alien to them."[2]

The artist Pablo Picasso is credited with having said, "It takes a long time to become young!" Picasso had discovered that only after a long life filled with at least as many downs as ups and failures as successes could one become not only wise but, like a child, truly innocent and free. Paradoxically, I was not young enough to know or experience the full meaning and liberating ramifications of the word *omnipresent* when I first heard it, but as I've grown "younger" through the years, I have come to realize its radical breadth and depth. God is not someone who has mastered the art of bilocation; rather, *God* is a word that refers to the sacred mystery that is the spiritual essence of all creation. In support of this notion, theologian Michael Himes claims, "The word 'God' functions like x in algebra. It is a stand-in for the ... absolute mystery which grounds and supports all that exists."[3]

Perhaps it is the child in us that knows the simple yet mind-boggling truth of God's omnipresence. This is what Jesus seems to indicate when, in addressing his followers, he said: "I bless you, Father, Lord of heaven and of earth, for hiding these things from the learned and the clever and revealing them to mere children" (Matthew 11:25). To posit that God is the omnipresent Ground of our being, a notion put forth by theologian Paul Tillich and popularized by Bishop John A. T. Robinson in his classic work *Honest to God*, is not an advanced theory that only the learned and clever can comprehend, but an attempt to move beyond the limits of conceptualization by affirming with child-like wonder that the reality of God is not spatial but spiritual.

No theological words or concepts, no religious gestures or rituals, are sufficient to express this mystery. I was reminded of this by a nun for whom I serve as a spiritual director. A woman who has grown younger throughout her fifty-plus years in the convent, Sister Miriam stated that one day, while making the sign of the cross (touching her forehead, chest, and both shoulders while saying "In the name of the Father, and of the Son, and of the Holy Spirit"), she had this childlike thought: "It's too small." Even the concept of the Trinity, about which tomes have been written, had become too confining for her experience of the infinite and intimate nature of God. As feeble as our attempts may be, the need to give expression both in word and gesture to our experience of the Divine is a powerful and positive instinct; however, it is important to remember that when we try to name the unnameable, we often end up limiting the limitless.

When I was first exposed to the idea of God beyond religion, I found it not only eye-opening but, in a sense, heartbreaking as well. I had had a relationship with God that was far more than a matter of belief, because I spoke to God, I sought solace in God, and I felt that, along with being protected, I was both known and loved by God. Although I now experience God's presence in a way that is more mysterious and yet more personal than was the case in my youth, letting go of the belief that God is an actual person has precipitated a process of grieving that, years later, I continue to feel from time to time. I still miss the old guy!

But just as it is necessary to exhale in order to inhale, I have found that, without letting go of my early notions of God, there could be no room in me for a new and more expansive understanding of Divinity or for the liberating way of life that flows from it—one that is free from the fear of a punitive God and free for an experience of God in the nitty-gritty of everyday life and relationships.

God's Death: A Necessary Demise

When I first read philosopher Friedrich Nietzsche's statement "God is dead," I was still filled with the comforting belief in God understood as a Supreme Being and was thus unable to take in the magnitude of this radical claim. But I now see that the death of the God I encountered within religion has been a necessary demise, one that has enabled me to breathe more deeply and to be filled more completely with the life of the Spirit.

My groping after the absolute and my stumbling upon it in the here and now have led me to conclusions that will be upsetting to some and were, in fact, troubling to me when I first articulated them. Like a person trying to find a position of comfort in bed, I have tossed and turned with them in the darkness of uncertainty for many years. However, I realize that as I have been reaching and, for the present, resting in these conclusions, God has become liberated from the confinement of my limited anthropomorphic notions. And I too have become liberated, not from confinement but from the concern for acceptability that comes with assuming that God is made in the likeness of humanity—loving and forgiving conditionally.

The conclusions I refer to are grounded in the apophatic tradition embodied in mystics like John of the Cross and Meister Eckhart. The Greek root of the word *apophatic* literally means "to deny." This perspective posits that God is not a person as we are people. It speaks of the no-thingness of God, the reality that no thought, feeling, or statement about God can come close to the spiritual reality that is God.

What now makes sense to my mind and heart is that there simply is no God who looks down upon us or our planet. There is no divine person who has a plan for our lives or our world, or who judges, rewards, or condemns us for not living up to his expectations. There is no Supreme Being somewhere in or beyond the universe who created creation. These statements are not a denial of the reality of God but a way of saying that the mystery to which the word *God* refers is beyond any image or concept. My conclusions have enabled me to affirm that the reality of God far exceeds my wildest imagination and some of religion's most cherished beliefs.

Having said this, I also need to state that the notion of God as a Supreme Being speaks to a very deep human need. We are fragile and contingent beings who find ourselves alive for a very brief time on the surface of a tiny sphere suspended in limitless space. Why are we here? How is it that we have come to be? What will become of us when we die? In the face of our smallness, we long for an ultimate and personal presence, someone who stands beyond our precariousness and in whom we can find both meaning and security. I believe that the idea of a Supreme Being has grown, in part, from this condition and need, for such a God can be a comforting companion in our vulnerability.

Belief in God as a being who gives us a sense of meaning and security is a good thing, for in their absence of meaning and security, aimlessness and fear would reign, thus making it impossible for us to live positive, productive lives. Such a belief is problematic only if we think God is who we think God is. God is always more than our theories and our theologies—even the one I am positing, which claims God is beyond theory and theology! No matter how much sense our notion of God makes to us, we must be willing to be confounded by the fact that no notion of God is God. When it comes to God, confusion, though far from clarity, may actually be closer to the truth.

Life after God Is Life with God

The belief that God is beyond religion (that the Infinite is intimate) has led to two very important changes that have made my life richer and more vital. The first is that I now walk the earth with a greater sense of the sacredness of everyday life. God is in everything, and everything is in God. Whether majestic or mundane, attractive or repulsive, profound or inconsequential, all things, people, and circumstances elicit in me a sense of reverence, for they are not apart from the holiness that permeates them. The prophet Isaiah gives voice to this truth when he claims on behalf of Yahweh, "Let it be known from East to West that apart from me there is no one" (Isaiah 45:6).

When I believed that God was a distant and Supreme Being who had a very definite set of preferences, I approached life conditionally. Some things, people, and events were to be embraced, and others were not. Spiritual endeavors were primary, while concerns of a physical or material nature ran a distant second. Saints were to be venerated, but sinners were to be scorned. And, to paraphrase an ancient hymn, where charity and love prevailed, there God was ever found. But when discord and hatred reigned, I presumed that God was missing in action.

While there is plenty of room for discerning between what is healthy and unhealthy, just and unjust, acceptable as it is and in need of change, I now realize that all dimensions of life's complexity are part of a holy wholeness. This concept was known to the author of the book of Ecclesiastes, who wrote, "There is a season for everything, a time for every occupation under heaven" (Ecclesiastes 3:1).

When we understand that nothing occurs apart from God, everything can be entered as a dimension of our journey with God. Even illness, war, poverty, and death are dimensions of the paradoxical sacredness of our less than perfect existence on this planet; for although they are not "intended" by God, they are part of the territory of human experience where God is to be discovered as a compassionate presence, one with us in our fear and pain. Life is no longer only sacred or secular, black or white; it is also a grace-filled gray.

Because this is so, I am challenged to cease doing what I have always done: battle with reality. Whether it's the weather I don't like, a task I'd rather not do, or a person who rubs me the wrong way, I often find myself resisting and resenting the reality of my life. I am convinced that I will go to my grave wanting life to be what I want it to be, but I am now certain that the whole messy lot of it is replete with holiness.

I am learning gradually to honor even those aspects of life that it is right to work toward eradicating, and to look reverently upon those whom I view as my enemies. While speaking to a group of people interested in both spirituality and social justice, Buddhist monk and peace activist Thich Nhat Hanh once said: "Never write a letter to a congressperson unless you can write a love letter." When I write, speak, or act without the love that flows from an awareness of God's presence in me and others, I am apt to become part of the problem I seek to correct. Only words and actions grounded in love embody the change that can bring about a more just and peace-filled world.

Another way in which my concept of God has changed the way I live is that I now think of all people as manifestations of God. I am in awe of the divinity of humanity and the humanity of divinity. The religious lines drawn hard, fast, and early in my life, lines that separated me from God, have now become a blessed blur. For me, the idea that we live in exile from God has given way to the realization that we are in a state of existential intimacy with the Divine; we could not be unless we were imbued with Being itself.

This is by no means something I experience a majority of the time. In the same way that I do not always feel love for or closeness to the people who matter most to me, I walk most days without a feeling of love of or closeness to God. But both affection and connection are real, whether felt or not. I take some consolation in the recent revelation that even Mother Teresa lived without a felt sense of God for much of her life.

In a letter published in *Mother Teresa: Come Be My Light*, she explained to Father Joseph Neuner:

> The place of God in my soul is blank.—There is no God in me.—When the pain of longing is so great just long and long for God—and that is when I feel—He does not want me—He is not there. ... You see ... the contradiction in my life. I long for God—I want to love Him—to love Him much—to live only for Love of Him—to love only—and yet there is but pain— longing and no love.[4]

God's Will: Blueprint or Imprint?

Because I believe that God is one with our humanity, I am challenged to cease doing something else I have always done: engage in negative self-talk. Like a moth drawn to the source of light, I am prone to flutter around self-negativity. I find it difficult to accept compliments and easy to assume that I am in the wrong. I lean instinctively toward what I consider my shortcomings and, in comparison to most others, be it in appearance, accomplishments, or intelligence, I usually consider myself second-rate. As with my penchant to want what I want, I am convinced that I will go to my grave with the tendency to judge myself harshly; however, I now realize that I am more than my assessment of myself, just as I am more than my roles and titles. Poet Roger Housden echoes this view in his commentary on Trappist monk and mystic Thomas Merton's poem "In Silence":

> Perhaps you already know that your true identity can never be described by your personal attributes, or by what you do in the world.... "I am a mother, a company director, a writer, an actor, a musician" rise only from our surface.[5]

I am certain that what is most true about me and all others is that we are "of God." To malign ourselves, no matter how imperfect we are, is a form of blasphemy, and to assume that we are worthwhile only because of what we do is to miss the godly nature of who we are.

Because I believe that our nature is awash with the divine, I now think of the term *God's plan* not as a blueprint but as an imprint. I do not have to conform to external dictates in order to please God; rather, I must be faithful to my soul-self in order to be true to God. Deep within each of us there resides a sacredness that is our essence. When I live in accord with this, when I am one with what Jungian analyst James Hillman calls the soul's code, I am in harmony with God and at peace with myself. I am, of course, free to live in such a way—busy and noisy—as to make myself impervious to the intuitive tugs that are the Spirit's way of nudging me toward integrity. But because I am in God and God is in me, I can, if I ignore such proddings, count on a healthy sense of guilt, a knock on the door of my conscience that calls me to be true to who I truly am: the "Hound of Heaven," pursuing us out of love, is relentless.

If this way of understanding God seems too individualistic, I must also state that it has made the reality of community more meaningful and powerful for me. My understanding of community under the purview of a Supreme Being was that everyone was essentially separate from everyone else but that we were "in it together." We needed one another to become our best selves and to come to right relationship with God, who was as apart from us as we were from each other.

But believing that Divinity and humanity are inseparable calls us to a more profound sense of relatedness to one another. Interdependence rather than independence or dependence becomes the way of right relationship, because what we are in together is the *within* (soul) of every person. Community in the deepest sense has to do not with our common identity based on ethnicity, shared beliefs, common experience, or any other unessential likeness, but with our spiritual makeup, the common godliness of our being.

I believe that not only the local communities we may be part of—family, neighborhood, work, church, and the like—would be stronger if everyone experienced God as their common denominator, but so would the community of humanity. Racism, sexism, ageism, war, and other such travesties rest on a foundation that is devoid of the awareness of Divinity's indwelling. When God is understood as an entity apart from reality, reality loses the glue that enables unity in the midst of diversity. But when God is recognized as the deepest dimension of our being, our differences can be seen for what they are:

not barriers that separate, but facets, like those of a diamond, reflecting the precious beauty of the gem.

At this point in my life I consider God to be the immensity of the minute, the eternality of the temporal, and the infinity of the finite. This understanding of God may seem too impersonal for some, but it helps me make sense of St. Augustine's claim that "God is closer to us than we are to ourselves."

Because it is cumbersome to do otherwise, in the chapters that follow, I will, often refer to God in ways that may seem to reinforce the traditional notion of a separate being. But in all cases, my hope is that you, dear reader, will realize that such language is both limited and misleading, for the reality of God, though vast beyond measure, is never apart from us.

Questions for Your Own Journey

What are your earliest impressions, thoughts, images, and feelings regarding God?

In what ordinary aspects of life do you stumble upon the Holy?

How has your concept of and relationship with God grown? What is your current view of God?

What are the catalysts that have influenced your concept of God?

⌒

2

What Becomes of Prayer If There Is No God?

> If prayer is the act of engaging God and if God is the
> source of life, then my prayer time became my time
> of engaging life. The monastic prayer pattern created
> by a theism that located God outside of life, an under-
> standing that suggested that one must withdraw from
> life to pray or to be holy, was turned upside down.
> —John Shelby Spong, *A New Christianity
> for a New World*

While I was speaking about God beyond religion to a group of retreatants, Sharon, a woman who was troubled by this notion, asked, "Why bother to pray if there is no one to pray to?" I've heard the same question, albeit expressed differently, many times: "If God is not someone who hears and answers prayers, why waste our breath asking, thanking, or praising him?" "Isn't it pointless to pray if there is no one to whom we can direct our prayers?"

I could feel the anxiety that gave birth to Sharon's question, for it is troubling to think that if God is not the Supreme Being we thought God was, our prayers might fall not on "deaf" ears but on no ears at all. In fact, Sharon's question was my question when my understanding of God began to grow beyond religion and as I took my first halting steps on the spiritual path. Before that, my understanding of prayer was formed according to the *Baltimore Catechism* definition: the lifting up of our minds and hearts to God.[1] This definition implies that being in touch with God requires us to focus our thoughts and feelings on a realm above our own. God is literally "out of this world."

Prayers Rather Than Prayer

I have always taken God and prayer seriously. In my Catholic tradition, praying in my own words was not stressed as much as the recitation and memorization of prayers like the Lord's Prayer, the Hail Mary, the Act of Contrition, and grace before and after meals. My prayers were mostly read and said; this is referred to as *discursive prayer*.

As a child I tried to think about and to mean each word of the prayers I recited, and if I became distracted, which was always the case, I would begin the prayer again. I believed that by doing so, I was pleasing God. The harder I tried to concentrate on the words I was saying and the more I fought off the thoughts and images that intruded on my piety, the more my mind drifted from my prayers. I haven't confirmed this, but I may be listed in the *Guinness Book of World Records* for taking the longest time to recite the Lord's Prayer!

Because I believed that God was a being who inhabited a faraway place, the prayers of my youth were aimed like arrows at a distant target. I knew I hit the bull's-eye when my prayers were answered, a notion learned from reading Matthew 6:6: "But whenever you pray, go into your room and shut the door and pray to your Father who is in secret; and your Father who sees in secret will reward you."

When I first began to practice a more contemplative form of prayer, I still believed I could "get it right." However, instead of returning to memorized words when my mind wandered, I tried to refocus my attention on my breathing or on a repetitive word or short phrase (a mantra) in the hope of stilling my mind and remaining in a meditative state. Although this form of prayer was very different from that of my youth, I continued to imagine that God was a separate being, and prayer continued to be a battleground wherein I fought the distractions that diverted my attention from the Divine. It was not until I encountered God beyond religion that I became more at ease about both God and prayer. It was then that I realized that I didn't have to lift my mind and heart away from life in order to be near God, and that nearness to God, not a mind free from distractions, was the essence of prayer.

Another Way to Pray

Because my beliefs about both God and prayer have evolved, I have come to the conclusion that the "Why bother to pray?" question is less meaningful than this query: "What becomes of prayer when we cease to envision God as a person?" This is a more useful question because it presumes not that prayer is pointless if there is no one to point it to but that a different concept of God invites us to a new understanding of prayer.

When we embrace God as the spiritual Ground of being, a reality that is a *part of* rather than *apart from* life, prayer can become more than those occasions when we intentionally think about or speak to God. Instead, prayer can be understood as the ongoing opening of our hearts to God present in ourselves, others, nature, circumstances, and events. When God is close at hand, prayer is more a matter of communion than communication.

On one of the monthly occasions when I meet with Glenn to speak about spiritual matters, he presented this dilemma: "In the evening, when my day has come to an end, I would like to pray, but instead I almost always choose to eat peanut butter!" In lieu of sitting quietly with a spiritual book, or practicing meditation, Glenn would fix himself a plate of peanut butter and crackers and feel guilty about not praying. In response to this I wondered out loud whether it might be possible to eat peanut butter prayerfully. I was not suggesting that Glenn shouldn't pray in a traditional manner or that he should think holy thoughts while eating peanut butter. I was offering instead the possibility that there is a way of eating, or doing anything, for that matter, that could be considered prayer. Though a bit of a stretch to the Western mind, this notion is familiar to Eastern thought and is expressed in the saying "Zen does not confuse spirituality with thinking about God while peeling potatoes. Spirituality *is* peeling potatoes!" Prayer is not necessarily a specific kind of activity but a wholehearted entry into whatever we do, for it is in this state of absorption that we can experience the stunning truth that materiality is spirituality incarnate.

Instead of lifting mind and heart away from creation in order to pray, I am now inclined to be as fully present to life as possible in order to commune with God hidden in its every nook and cranny. Retired Episcopal bishop John Shelby Spong has written of a similar transformation in his understanding and practice of prayer:

> In the more traditional and theistic phase of my life, I developed a habit of spending the first two hours of the day ... in prayer and study. I would pray first for those nearest and dearest to me....
>
> Then I would go through the world's trouble spots, praying for peace and for the end of suffering in war-torn lands.... Finally, I would go over the things I had to do that day, bringing both people and events into my prayer focus....
>
> As I moved beyond theism into a post-theistic understanding of God, I discovered that my commitment to starting my day with this focused two-hour time slot did not change, but my understanding of what I was doing did....

Prayer became for me the way I lived, loved, and struggled, the way I dared to be. Preparation for prayer was the time I spent in my office each morning recalling who I am, remembering where God is and how God can be met.[2]

I will address the importance of what Spong refers to as "preparation for prayer" at the end of this chapter, but for now I would like to focus on what he came to realize: that preparatory prayer is in the service of living prayerfully—with a readiness to be smitten by the divinity of simple things in the midst of our daily duties.

Prayer As Appreciation

How can we live so as not to miss God manifest in the details of our work, our leisure, our relationships? How must we live if life is to be a prayer? What is it that St. Paul had in mind when he encouraged us to "pray without ceasing"? (1 Thessalonians 5:17).

My answer to these questions is the simple word *appreciation*. By *appreciation* I do not mean gratitude; being thankful for life does not make the living of it a prayer. Appreciation can be recognized as an essential element of a prayerful life when understood as a derivative of the two Latin words *ad pretium*, meaning "go to the precious." When we go to the precious, to what is most valuable, to the sacred core, to the spiritual essence of life, then our every act, no matter how mundane, can become an encounter with God, who is that essence. Thomas Merton says this playfully when he writes: "What I wear is pants. What I do is live. How I pray is breathe."[3] Whether we are making dinner or making love, driving a car or staring at a star, breathing in or breathing out, we are on the thin ice through which we might just plunge into the precious, sacred abyss of the numinous nature of ordinary life.

When we fall through the ice—that is, when we intuitively sense the sacredness at the heart of life—we come to realize that any sense of separation from God, understood as the Ground of being, is an illusion. Because this is true and because, from a contemplative perspective, prayer is being in communion with God, it follows that every moment of our lives can be considered prayerful. Psychologist and Merton scholar James Finley refers to our closer-than-close union with God when he writes:

> In passing from ego consciousness to meditative states of awareness, we are awakened to that eternal oneness with God that *is* the very reality of ourselves and of everyone and everything around us.[4]

This way of being in the world is not my normal manner of living, for meditative consciousness senses the subtle presence of the Divine in the midst of our daily life and our very selves. What is normal for me and, I believe, for most of us, is to live in ego consciousness. Here we look at life with eyes that judge it to be beautiful or repugnant, useful or useless, pleasurable or painful, and so on. From a practical perspective, it is important to view life in this way, for we need to make decisions based on judgments like these many times a day. Everything from crossing the street, deciding what to have for dinner, or choosing to whom we will reveal our fears and vulnerability situates us in ego consciousness.

But spiritually speaking, when we fail to experience life at a deeper level, we fail to encounter its divinity. When we truly meet life, we meet God meeting us. An appreciative heart, attuned to the divinity of life, would surely make our often burdensome and tedious lives more meaningful and prayerful, because when we are present to the moment, we are present to the Presence that is the mystery of God incarnate in creation.

Living with prayerful appreciation means going to the precious stillness that gives birth to all motion, resting in the sacred silence from which all sound arises, and intuiting the spiritual no-thingness that underlies all things. It becomes possible to sense the divine depths of life when we pause from activity, listen to the sounds of silence with what St. Benedict refers to as the "ear of our heart," and open our souls to that which cannot be known with our minds. To me, this is prayer at its most expansive and all-encompassing best. It is prayer freed from the limits of praying only in formal ways and at specific times. This prayer is the living of our lives with the conviction that God is here (in the world) and not just there (in heaven). It is the openness of our soul to the truth that God is not just within us, but that God *is* the "within" of us. God is not just where we are, but who we are at one with wherever we are.

When we live from this only sometimes felt but always present truth, we live with the innocence of the squirrel that, as I write, is perched precariously on a branch outside my window. As it leaps from branch to branch, tree to tree, and tree to fence, the squirrel is not concerned about precarious circumstances but lives, instead, in total trust of its nature, as did the birds of the air and the wildflowers that Jesus referred to when he encouraged his followers to be more trustful:

> Therefore I tell you, do not worry about your life, what you will eat or what you will drink, or about your body, what you will wear. Is not life more than food, and the body more than clothing? Look at the birds of the air; they neither sow nor reap nor gather into barns, and yet your heavenly Father feeds them. Are you not of more value than they? And can any of you by worrying add a single hour to your span of life? And why do you worry about clothing? Consider the lilies of the field, how they grow; they neither toil nor spin, yet I tell you, even Solomon in all his glory was not clothed like one of these. But if God so clothes the grass of the field, which is alive today and tomorrow is thrown into the oven, will he not much more clothe you—you of little faith? (Matthew 6:25–30)

How differently—and prayerfully—most of us would live if we focused on the preciousness within; that is, if we trusted the divinity of our human nature. How much more spontaneously we would go about our days free from worry, not only about what others might think of us but even about what God, understood as a Supreme Being, might think. These are concerns that place us, not God, at the center of our spiritual lives. Buddhist psychologist and author Jack Kornfield writes about spiritual maturity as self-forgetfulness and the freedom to enter the everyday reality of our lives:

> With spiritual maturity the basis ... shifts away from ambition, idealism, and desire for self-transformation. It is as if the wind has changed, and a weather vane— still centered in the same spot—now points in a different direction: back to this moment. We are no longer striving for a spiritual destination....We are home. And being home, we sweep the floor, make nourishing meals, and care for our guests.[5]

Prayer As Immersion in the Moment

Living prayerfully becomes a reality when we let go of preoccupying concerns—even those of a religious or spiritual nature— and immerse ourselves in who and what is before us in the present moment.

I recall learning the lesson that prayer is about immersion in the moment during the first of many retreats I have made at Genesee Abbey, a Trappist monastery near Rochester, New York. I went there in the summer of 1975 in order to prepare myself for the new direction my life was taking: I was leaving my ministry at the University of Notre Dame and was going to begin studies in spirituality in Berkeley, California. I arranged to spend three weeks at the monastery, during which I chose to enter the routine of monastic life as fully as possible. This involved rising in time to chant the psalms and listen to sacred readings at Vigils, which began at 2:25 a.m. This was the first of five such gatherings for common prayer—Lauds, Sext, Vespers, and Compline being the others. At the close of Vigils there was a period of quiet reflection, during which I usually fell asleep. After Lauds, which began at 5:00 a.m., I worked in the bakery three days a week—the community at Genesee produces thousands of loaves of Monk's Bread each week as a means of self-support. My stint in the bakery was followed by the first of two work periods, each of which lasted two to three hours (manual labor is one of the three pillars of monastic life—prayer and study are the others—and is a major part of every day except Sunday). Vespers and the Eucharist were celebrated after work; the day ended with Compline at 6:40 p.m.

After three weeks of this routine, I realized that I did not have the time for contemplative prayer that I had anticipated and that I thought characterized monastic life. I expected to have frequent periods of extended time for meditation, reflection, and spiritual reading, but so strenuous was the life and work of the monks that I was too tired to pray when the opportunities for doing so presented themselves. As I paused to reflect on this situation, I realized that I must learn to pray while chanting the psalms, in the midst of the work in the bakery and in the fields, while eating, and during the half-mile walk between the retreat house and the Abbey church. I became aware that there was a way to understand prayer that made it the thread woven into every activity, every encounter, and every moment of a monk's life, and that this could be the case in my life beyond the cloistered confines of the monastery.

I have found appreciation and immersion in the moment to be nothing short of a profound way to understand and to enter prayer. But because there are many people who find this too impersonal, I would now like to consider prayer using the analogy of a personal relationship.

Prayer As Relationship

I first began to think about prayer relationally some years ago while visiting with a friend in Chicago. Ann was talking about her then-boyfriend, now-husband, Jim, and about how they spent many of their weekends. Some of the time they spent together, some of it apart. Even when they were together, there were times when they were in their own worlds, not conversing with each other or sharing common endeavors. They were two separate people whose lives and activities unfolded in the context of a bond of love. They were together, one in their relationship, even when they were apart and without consciousness of each other.

As Ann spoke, I was struck by the awareness that what she was describing was a metaphor for prayer or, better yet, for living prayerfully. As I have already mentioned, I learned that prayer was intentional time with God—a time of intense concentration wherein we sit either in stillness, not clinging to any thoughts or feelings (contemplative prayer), or in a conscious articulation in thoughts or words of needs, gratitude, or praise (discursive prayer). Although there is immense value in these forms of prayer, I believe that real prayer is at heart a relationship. It is the living of our everyday lives in communion with God, who is the Ground of our lives, the ever-present Other who is not other than who we are, the center around which our lives turn, the Mystery that is given form in and through our person.

For all of us, this is a relationship that is every bit as real as that of any two people in love. There is a reality at the center of ourselves around which our days unfold and from which we are never parted. All of our comings and goings, ordinary as they may be, are lived in a relationship of oneness with this Sacred Life Source. We need not be conscious of this for it to be the case, any more than two people in love need to be constantly conscious of each other in order to remain in relationship. The reality of who they are to each other is a given, and so is the truth that we are inseparable from God.

For Ann and Jim, there has been a growing trust in the significance each has in the life of the other—this has formed the foundation that allows them the freedom to just live, to be with each other and to be apart, to go about the tasks at hand, and to respond to the demands of the day, wherever that takes them, separately or together.

In any healthy relationship, each of us gives and in return, feels a freedom that allows us to just live and be who we are. There is such a freedom in relation to God. We are called to trust in the communion with God that has given birth to us, sustains us, and summons us to wholeness. We are invited to be present to the moment, the people, and the tasks at hand, confident that all we do is somehow a dimension of who we are in God. The relationship is intact, even when we are not thinking about or attending to it.

A relationship is on shaky ground if either party is reluctant to trust the other. If in our intentional times of prayer we do not trust that God's love is unconditional, our prayer is likely to be awkward and self-conscious. It will feel like something we should do rather than a natural expression of and appreciation for a life-giving bond. In such a case, we may fall prey to the tendency to measure the quality of our prayer—the fewer the distractions, the more peaceful the feeling, the more lofty the insights, the better. This attitude will surely lead to discouragement, for who among us emerges from intentional times of prayer having consistently succeeded in attaining these outcomes? But if we know in our hearts that "nothing can separate us from the love of God" (Romans 8:39), distractions during prayer will not be a matter of great concern.

Intentional Prayer

I have tried to make the point that prayer in the fullest sense is more than thoughts or words addressed to God in the quiet of our hearts or, for that matter, in a worshipping assembly. But in order to nourish our relationship with God, times of intentional prayer (what Bishop Spong refers to as preparation for prayer)—moments when we step aside from the pushes and pulls of life to speak, to listen, to praise, and to rest in God—are crucial. Such times are as significant in relation to our spiritual lives as intimacy of every sort is to loving interpersonal relationships.

I was reminded of the importance of intentional prayer while speaking with a friend recently. Phil is in his late fifties and has a high-powered job managing the egos of the CEOs on the board of a prominent charitable organization. Phil meditates regularly. He spends several twenty-minute periods every day sitting in silence. "When I meditate," he said, "I can go into stressful meetings and remain calm; I can deal respectfully with the people there, even the ones I don't like. But when I miss a few days in a row, I'm a bastard!"

Without the discipline of making time to intentionally engage God within ourselves, we run the risk of drifting from the awareness that we are always in communion with God. And without the discipline of celebrating God's presence with others, we are at risk of losing touch with the spiritual bond that unites us to humankind. But the good news is that even when we fail to do this—when we forget, could not care less, are angry at or in other ways feel estranged from God—we still remain in God. Recalling this truth when we find ourselves being "bastards" can bring us back to a respectful and reverent way of relating to others and to ourselves.

To say that the God of theism does not exist doesn't make prayer irrelevant, for when God is freed from the limits of being a being, both God and prayer take on new meaning. Then the notion of God becomes limitless, everywhere present and from nowhere absent. And because we are in a state of constant communion with God, both within and outside ourselves, prayer can be considered more than an activity consisting of words or thoughts directed to God. Instead, our entire lives can be a prayer, a liturgy celebrating the presence of God incarnate in every breath we take, every word we utter, and every movement we make.

Questions for Your Own Journey

How did you pray when you were a child, and what did you expect from the act of praying?

How do you know when your prayers are answered, and how do you explain it when they are not?

How has your prayer practice changed since you were a child? How does the notion of appreciation or presence as a form of prayer resonate with your personal prayer practice?

What aspects of interpersonal relationships do you experience as a dimension of prayer?

3

From Belief to Faith

The Greek term for *faith* is the same one often inter-
preted simply as *belief*, since faith often *includes* belief,
but it involves much more: the trust that enables us to
commit ourselves to what we hope and love.... Most
of us, sooner or later, find that, at critical points in
our lives, we must strike out on our own to make a
path where none exists.

—Elaine Pagels, *Beyond Belief*

It has been said that the fact that you are not dead is not sufficient proof that you are alive. Whenever I repeat this saying
at retreats or workshops, there is always a ripple of knowing
laughter. Most people can identify with it. Many of us realize
that having opted for an existence characterized by the likes of
comfort, routine, and security has resulted in our being less than
fully alive. This state of quasi-vitality can be a reality not only
personally and professionally but spiritually as well.

As I reflect on my life, it is clear to me that like a biker rid-
ing downhill, I coasted comfortably for years, believing the
teachings of my faith tradition without question and obeying its
rules without protest. As a child, I memorized the questions and
answers in the *Baltimore Catechism*. As an adolescent, I tried to

meet the moral standards of qualification for being a good boy. In the seminary, I lived by the adage "You keep the rule, and the rule will keep you." There were, however, times when I lived by a different saying: "It's easier to ask for forgiveness than for permission!"

I thought it virtuous at the time, but I now see that my compliance was a way of fitting in and of winning the respect of both my peers and my elders. I was not growing spiritually, but merely hoping to meet the requirements that ensured me the acceptance of others and, of course, the approval of God. I was playing my cards right and therefore had the attitude Mark Twain spoke of when he referred to the calm confidence of a Christian with four aces! Although I believed what I was supposed to and did what I was told, I did not have the winning hand of faith—that is, the willingness to trust in God and the courage to live with holy abandon. I was not dead, but neither was I spiritually alive.

The formulation of what I was taught to believe is contained in the Nicene Creed, one outcome of the First Council of Nicea, a conclave convened in 325 CE by the Christian convert and emperor Constantine. The Creed is a statement of belief in, among other things, God as the Father Almighty and Jesus as "God from God, Light from Light, true God from true God." Aligning oneself with these truths and others is nonnegotiable if one is to be considered Christian.

Questioning Beliefs, Affirming Faith

The capacity to believe is important, for there is much in life that is deflating and defeating without it. Belief in others, even though they disappoint us, can salvage damaged relationships. Belief in ourselves, even though we fail to practice what we preach or settle for mediocrity, can help us achieve our goals when throwing in the towel is more appealing than perseverance. And belief in God can sustain us throughout our lives, especially during times of trial.

Because belief is so powerful and empowering, I felt a sense of uncertainty when what I once believed began to lose meaning. As I started my trek along the spiritual path, I pondered many previously unquestioned beliefs—for example, that God would intervene to protect us from harm, that Jesus was sent to die for our sins, and that only those who believed in Jesus as the Son of God would be saved. Because I grappled with, and in some cases rejected, what I had believed, I felt adrift, uncertain whether anything would replace those beliefs. I now recognize that this crisis was a dark gift—a blessing in disguise—for my confusion was the beginning of a spiritual maturity that has led me to the realization that I can live with faith even when I no longer believe all that I was taught.

Before proceeding any further, I want to clarify the distinction between the words *belief* and *faith* as I am using them and to state that by contrasting them, I am not implying that they are oppositional. Religious belief is generally considered a matter of the mind (*assensus*)—what I believe is what I give assent to, what I hold to be true. Faith, in contrast, is about not holding onto anything; true faith is a matter of trust (*fiducia*), of letting go—not of my beliefs, necessarily, but of my reluctance to give myself to God. Faith is not a body of beliefs but a way of living, putting my body where my beliefs are.

Do I stop at the doorway of believing that the Israelites wandered through the desert for forty years, or do I find in this biblical epic the courage to traverse the wasteland of uncertainty that is my life from time to time? Do I rest content in the belief that God became incarnate in Jesus, or do I daily embrace the God-Self that I am and others are? Do I merely believe that Jesus's death was life-giving, or do I die to my will, my preferences, and my way, when doing so might benefit others? Am I satisfied with believing that Jesus was raised from the dead, or do I open myself to the Spirit's life-giving power, calling me from the graves of lethargy, fear, and insecurity?

The difference between belief and faith is illustrated in a story about a tightrope walker in a circus. The crowd was mesmerized when he walked across the wire without a balance pole, when he walked blindfolded, and when he pushed a wheelbarrow from one platform to the other. When his act was over, the crowd called for more. He asked what they wanted him to do, and someone shouted, "The wheelbarrow."

"Do you have faith that I can do it again?" he asked.

"Yes," the audience member replied.

"In that case," he said, "get in!"

It is one thing to believe from a distance and another to get in the wheelbarrow—that is, to go for the ride of a lifetime, to entrust ourselves to God.

Believing can be safe, but faith is risky. Believing can be comfortable, while faith is challenging. Religious beliefs often affirm that something has happened (as in the life of Jesus), while faith is openness to what is *happening*. Faith has less to do with history than with mystery—present, alive, and enlivening.

Religious beliefs may lead us to enter temples, churches, mosques, and synagogues, but it is faith that sends us out the door to engage life with the values our religion espouses. We celebrate our beliefs with those who share them in buildings designated as sacred, but we practice our faith at home, at work, and in our relationships with all people on the sacred ground that is the earth.

Because religious truths are meant to enhance the quality and character of our daily lives, they should be related to with the whole heart, not merely believed with the mind. Christian theologian Marcus Borg writes about the impotence of mere beliefs:

> You can believe all the right things and still be in bondage. You can believe all the right things and still be miserable. You can believe all the right things and still be relatively unchanged. Believing a set of claims to be true has very little transforming power.[1]

Affirming religious beliefs without being open to the transformation they call us to is like acknowledging the importance of communication in a relationship without willing to grapple with the potentially growthful challenges that come with closeness to another. Faith invites us to engage in life, not just to theorize about it.

I now know that belief is to faith what meditation is to contemplation; the latter, in each case, is the end, the fulfillment of the former. Meditation understood as thinking about God is itself a good thing, but this type of prayer is meant to be a doorway to a contemplative and intimate experience of God. Believing in the reality, love, and power of God is important in our development as full spiritual beings, but surrendering to the immediacy of the power of God's love is what can empower us to act in ways that enhance our own and others' lives. Faith gives flesh to our beliefs.

Seeing with Eyes of Faith

Faith challenges us to open ourselves to the truth that there is virtue in the sometimes childlike way we stumble through life. The heart of each of the parents I know has been pierced by the preciousness of his or her young child's mispronounced words and bumbling first steps. When we see the world, ourselves, and others with the eyes of faith, we behold grace and beauty even in what our body's eyes see as flawed.

Can it be that in our less-than-ideal state we are one with God? Is it paradoxically possible that our failure to "get it right" may be better than perfection? My answer to these questions is an unequivocal yes. In my own journey from belief to faith, and in accompanying others in their unsuccessful struggles to reach perfection, I have become convinced that it is only when we let go of our notions about what makes for holiness that we become free of the self-preoccupation that blinds us to the awareness that even now we live, move, and have our being in God.

George, one of the people for whom I serve as a spiritual direc-tor, is a wonderful person who has been a priest for many years. He works hard—perhaps too hard—at being the kind of virtuous person he learned he must be in order to please God. He spoke to me about being upset with the fact that he enjoyed the affirma-tion he received from the people he served. George believed that he should be more humble—that is, less affected by praise (or criticism) and more content with just doing his job, neither need-ing nor wanting to be shown appreciation for his efforts.

A traditional understanding of humility would support George's belief. I learned that humble people took no pride in their accomplishments and that they let compliments roll off their Teflon-like egos without having an effect, as in Matthew 6:1–4:

> Beware of practicing your piety before others in order
> to be seen by them; for then you have no reward from
> your Father in heaven.
>
> So whenever you give alms, do not sound a trumpet
> before you, as the hypocrites do in the synagogues and in
> the streets, so that they may be praised by others. Truly
> I tell you, they have received their reward. But when you
> give alms, do not let your left hand know what your right
> hand is doing, so that your alms may be done in secret;
> and your Father who sees in secret will reward you.

I suggested to George that a different understanding of humil-ity might be that there is nothing more humbling than to fail at being humble! In other words, the acceptance of the need to be affirmed involves the humble embrace of our less-than-ideal self. Acceptance of this sort requires faith understood as the sur-render of our notion of what it means to be virtuous and trust that who we are is good enough in God's eyes.

Faith and Confidence

When we let go of our efforts to please God and instead learn to trust God, we can begin to live with confidence—*confides*, with faith. When we surrender to the power of God's presence and action in our lives, we can live with confidence in the face of our fears, insecurities, and life's many difficult and dark times. When we get in the wheelbarrow, we are carried across abysses that we could never traverse on our own. When we open our hearts to the Spirit that dwells within, we encounter God incarnate in life.

The faith that enables us to live with confidence is a faith that has been nurtured and deepened, not one that lies dormant within a matrix of religious beliefs. During the early years of my priesthood I worked with Father Bill Toohey, who was the director of campus ministry at the University of Notre Dame throughout the 1970s. Bill, always a persuasive preacher, used to shock the parents of the freshman class at the beginning of each school year when he would address them on behalf of the faculty and administration, saying, "We do not promise to preserve your daughter's or son's faith during the years they will spend here." After pausing to let this statement sink into the minds and hearts of couples spending a small fortune to educate their children at a Catholic university, he would continue, "To promise this would be to promise far too little. What we do promise is that we will do all we can to *promote* their faith."

Conventional religious teaching posits that the preservation of faith (misunderstood as beliefs) from womb to tomb is a goal to strive for; to question or to doubt is an indication that one's faith is weak. St. Paul supports this when he claims that in reference to Abraham's being told he would become a father in his old age, "He never questioned or doubted God's promise" (Romans 4:20). But the preservation of true faith would be its demise, because faith is a way of living and of giving ourselves to God incarnate in the people and events that make up our lives.

It is a sign of stagnant faith when in the name of God and with the Bible as a proof text, one person condemns another because she or he is gay. It is an arrested faith that allows us to refuse to hear the cry of the poor. It is a childish faith that gives us a sense of superiority over people of other religious traditions. The preservation of faith does to the soul what the lack of exercise does to the body—both of them atrophy. But the promotion of faith, which is achieved in part by the willingness to question our beliefs, serves to strengthen us and to make us aware of our communion with and responsibility for one another.

Jesus spoke of the power of faith when he said, "If your faith were the size of a mustard seed, you could say to this mountain, 'Move from here to there,' and it would move. Nothing would be impossible for you" (Matthew 17:20). True faith, it seems, is a matter not of quantity but of quality. The mustard seed that is the willingness to open ourselves to the power of the Spirit is all that God needs to bring about good things in us and through us. This is evident in many of the gospel's healing stories, in which Jesus indicates that people's faith makes them whole. This suggests that any healings he may have performed were not so much magical as they were mutual, for healing and wholeness of body and soul are best facilitated when we are in touch with our spiritual strength. Because God is within, healing, like happiness, is an inside job.

Faith and Healing

There is a difference between faith that heals and faith healing. The former has to do with tapping into our souls and calling upon the Spirit that enables us to enter fully into life's trials. This may not affect the physical curing of our illness or the eradication of an unjust situation, but it can bring about a sense of wholeness and power that makes a positive difference in how we deal with both illness and injustice. Faith healing, in contrast, is ceding our power to another who promises, in the name of God, to cure what ails us or remove what oppresses us.

In my work as a hospital chaplain, I have encountered thousands of people who were ill, but I have never observed faith healing—that is, the overcoming of illness by the power of another's prayer or touch. However, I have often witnessed the healing power of faith, prayer, and touch. I have seen people, buoyed by the prayerful support and the hands-on presence of others, take on disease and disability based on their acceptance of the truth that God meets us in our brokenness.

When I was young, I believed that God was by my side when health, victory, happiness, and the like had the upper hand. And I learned to assume that when the opposite was the case—when life was painful or unfair—God, who had the power to protect me from such things, was absent. As the psalmist says, "Awake! Why are you asleep, O Lord? Why do you hide your face, forgetting our woe and our oppressions?" (Psalm 44:23–24).

But true faith invites us beyond a belief system that claims God is present only when life is good. It challenges us to embrace pain as well as pleasure and darkness as well as light, for faith claims that God is present not only in the best of times but also in the worst. When we are open to the Divine in the midst of our dis-ease, there can be peace beneath pain, joy in the midst of sadness, and, at times, healing that boggles the medical mind.

Faith and Discernment

Faith is required to live in response to the Spirit's lead, for the journeys we are called to embark upon—those sometimes frightful leave-takings and meanderings—often pit us against the current of acceptable behavior according to people and institutions we respect. In his book *Ten Poems to Change Your Life*, Roger Housden begins with a consideration of his fellow poet Mary Oliver's work, titled "The Journey." This is a powerful poem that speaks of listening to the voice within that calls us to be true to ourselves and to act as we must, despite what Oliver refers to as "bad advice." Housden elaborates on this in terms of faith:

> The true journey of your life *requires* a kind of madness. After all, from the standpoint of your old life,

you may be throwing everything away for nothing.
... You cannot plan for this sort of journey because
the entire undertaking relies on the unreasonableness
of faith. Faith is unreasonable because it rests on no
tangible evidence. It is beyond even belief.[2]

Without faith, we can die without ever having lived. We might
be applauded for being "faithful" to what we were taught was
God's way, but all the while we may have turned from God,
whose "word" sometimes challenges us to live a life of contra-
diction (against the word) in relation to familial, societal, and
religious conventions.

Faith of this sort is concrete, practical, and sometimes
painfully personal. Before making the decision to resign from
the religious life, I spent several weeks at the Cenacle Retreat
Center in Chicago's Lincoln Park neighborhood. While there,
I reflected on "The Journey" and on the other poems in
Housden's book. As the weeks passed, it became clear to me
that despite the unreasonableness of leaving the security of
life in a religious community, despite disappointing those who
were attached to my being their priest, and despite my own
predictable fears about making it in the world, I had to trust
the intuition that continued to prod me toward a new life. As I
write these words, the emotional process involved in this leave-
taking is still unfolding. I have had countless dreams and many
misgivings about my decision, but when I reflect on it in terms
of faith, it continues to be the only path on which I feel I am
walking with God.

The Gift of Doubt

Before concluding this chapter on belief and faith, I think it is
important to mention that there is a middle ground between
them—the proverbial desert of doubt. This was not considered
holy ground in the tradition in which I was raised. Doubters or
skeptics were only one rung up the ladder from nonbelievers;

they may not have qualified for hell, but that hot spot was visible from where they stood.

I am convinced that doubt can be spiritually healthy. Questioning our beliefs may be a sign that we are growing and searching, not content to accept answers that do not fit life's questions. Doubt is not the opposite of faith but a stage in its dynamic development, as philosopher Alfred North Whitehead contends:

> Religion is the transition from God the Void to God the Enemy, and from God the Enemy to God the Companion. Only with the death of our previous image can a new and more adequate one arise. Thus "substantive doubt" is a part of the life of faith.[3]

Doubt is not the road on which everyone travels toward a deeper faith, but it has been the one along which I have journeyed. I am now at a point in my life where I have a bigger problem with unquestioned answers than with unanswered questions. The former, like a period at the end of a sentence, indicates that the matter is closed. The latter, like a question mark, invites further conjecture and therefore the possibility of new understanding.

The willingness to question the answers provided by my childhood beliefs has made me more open, passionate, and compassionate toward others and more gentle and forgiving toward myself. By questioning the conventional beliefs of Catholicism, I have come to see more clearly and embrace more fully the reality of God as benevolently incarnate in life, in relationships, and in religions other than the one in which I am rooted. I no longer think that I have the right answers to life, but I now feel that I am asking the important questions and that I am more comfortable living in the "cloud of unknowing," that contemplative state of being that encourages resting in the "blind stirring of love."

An indication that we are moving from belief to faith is that we begin to live *confides*. When we grow beyond the limiting beliefs that make us afraid to give ourselves to life, we are positioning ourselves to trust more in God, and in our God-Self. For many of us, doubt has fueled this process and made it possible to, in the words of the epigraph for this chapter, "strike out on our own to make a path where none exists."[4]

Questions for Your Own Journey

What religious teachings, those you learned through a specific religion or church, do you no longer believe, and why?

How would you articulate the distinction between belief and faith in your own words? How it is similar to or different from the distinction described in this chapter?

What role, if any, has doubt or questioning played in bringing you to your current beliefs about religious truths? What role, if any, has it played in deepening your spiritual life?

If faith is a way of living involving trust in God, life, and love, do you consider yourself a person of faith? Why or why not?

⌒—

4

Jesus: The Way, or in the Way?

That Jesus is the only Son of God, born of a virgin; that he died for our sins; that he rose physically from the dead; that he will come again; and so forth. This image of Jesus no longer works for millions of people, both within and outside the church. For these millions, its literalism and exclusivity are not only unpersuasive, but a barrier to being Christian.
—Marcus Borg, *The Heart of Christianity*

"When you meet the Buddha on the road, kill him" is an iconoclastic adage that the followers of all religious traditions would do well to take seriously. This is not meant literally, of course, but as a way of saying that when we put someone on the proverbial pedestal of adulation, his or her radiance may make us blind to both his or her humanness and our holiness. Having grown up a Catholic, I put Jesus on a pedestal, so it is my notion of him that I must reconsider if I am to truly see who he was and what he reveals about us.

Looking at Jesus as he was presented to me in the gospels and through the teachings of the church was like looking at the sun; I was blinded by his light. What I learned about his divinity made it difficult to see his humanity. The Jesus I met on the road of my early religious journey was the Messiah, the promised savior that Jews had been waiting for throughout their history. He was the only Son of God, born of a virgin, and sent to atone for our sins. He suffered, died, was resurrected, and ascended to heaven. During the years of his public life, he taught, worked miracles, and supposedly founded a new religion (a commonly held misconception).

According to my faith tradition, being a follower of Jesus meant not only believing all that was taught about him, but also imitating the way he lived. Discipleship required a willingness to serve others, of course, but also to die to one's self: "If anyone wants to be a follower of mine, let him renounce himself and take up his cross and follow me" (Matthew 16:24).

I grew up with an "except Jesus" way of thinking and believing. Everyone made mistakes except Jesus. Everyone got sick except Jesus. Everyone had times of confusion, doubt, cynicism, and so on except Jesus; neither headache nor heartache ever made his life miserable. I was taught that Jesus was fully God and fully human, but the impression I had was more like 80/20 in favor of God. He may have looked like his peers, but his DNA was definitely divine. Granted, the gospels toss a bone to his humanity—he got angry at the money changers in the Temple (Luke 19:45), was moved by the death of his friend Lazarus (John 11:35), and balked at the prospect of dying on a cross (Matthew 26:39). But from his virginal birth to his bodily resurrection and ascension, he is, by and large, literally and figuratively presented as having walked on water.

I realize that it was not the intention of the evangelists to portray Jesus as one who was like the rest of us. They were attempting to convince others that he was the Messiah and therefore like no one else. Still, I think it is unfortunate that the gospels do not give us a more complete, more human picture of him that does not gloss over faults, foibles, or idiosyncrasies he

may have had. If Jesus were presented in this way (more flaw-
fully human), it might be easier for us to embrace the truth that
being human is not an impediment to being spiritual.

Seeing Jesus Anew

For decades, I was content with believing that Jesus was larger
than life. There was no question in my mind that in his divinity he was different from any person who had lived or would
ever live. This perspective of Jesus—sent from above, born of
a virgin, with emphasis on his divinity—is considered "high
Christology," the traditional teaching of Christian churches.
But in the aftermath of the Second Vatican Council, when much
that had been unthinkingly accepted about Catholic teaching
and practice came under scrutiny, I became aware that another,
more human way of seeing Jesus was emerging. As I read and
spoke with others about these revelations, I noticed that something deep within me was aroused. My inclination to worship
him as one who was above and beyond what we could ever
become gave way to a sense of warmth and wonder at how like
him we are, even with our flaws. I began to look upon Jesus as
my brother and teacher, as a social and political prophet as well
as a religious figure, and as one who may have been less than
perfect himself but no less divine because of that.

Seeing Jesus in all his earthly humanity is considered "low
Christology" and was popularly portrayed in the controversial
best-selling novel *The Da Vinci Code*. The book and the film based
on it posit that Jesus was married to, and had children with,
Mary Magdalene and that she had a prominent place among his
apostles. Though shocking to traditionalists, this take on Jesus
poses no threat to the faith of some or to Jesus's divine status.
In fact, for many Christians, this view affirms the dignity of
women, marriage, and humanity in general.

One of the ways I came to appreciate the sacredness of
Jesus's humanity was through the 1970s musical *Godspell*. I had
been ordained a priest only two months when a road company

of actors from New York came to South Bend, Indiana, to put on several performances of the play. I was enthralled by the touching mix of humor and pathos with which Jesus and his band of followers was portrayed. The vitality that the almost exclusively Jewish cast conveyed to the audience had the kind of effect on me that I believe Jesus had on his disciples—namely, to paraphrase the signature song from the play, a desire to see God more clearly, to love God more dearly, and to follow God more nearly, day by day.

As an aside, I came to know the cast members and to witness their performances in five different cities in the months following their stint in South Bend. I became a groupie! What took place for me in my informal interactions with these talented actors paralleled what was happening in my relationship with Jesus: both they and he were becoming more real to me. I was seeing, learning about, and coming to love the individuals they were beneath the roles they played.

My *Godspell* experience, my study of Christology, and my exposure to the writings of Jesus scholar Marcus Borg have brought me to the point where I no longer look up to Jesus as someone who is essentially different from the rest of us. Instead, I see him as a man who was conceived and born in the same sensual, sexual, and sacred manner as every person before and since. I believe he struggled with and rejoiced in the same things every Jewish boy did in his culture, but I also believe that he gradually grew to understand and experience an intimacy with God that was exceptional and that fueled the radical nature of his words and work.

I believe it was his awakening to the divinity of his humanity—and ours—and the totality with which he gave himself to this breathtaking truth that marks Jesus's significance in human history. He was not the scapegoat chosen to shoulder the burden of our misdeeds or the lamb slaughtered so that we would be spared God's wrath. These notions should not be taken literally, but ought to be viewed for what they are: stories borrowed from Jewish lore that were projected onto Jesus by his followers.

I consider Jesus to be my Lord (the one whose values I share and whose example and teachings I follow) not because he alone is God's son but because he embodied the truth that God is incarnate in every person and because he has revealed the grace-filled way of life that follows from this—one that is often referred to as the freedom of the children of God. And I consider Jesus to be our savior not because he has made heaven accessible to us after we die but because he has liberated us here and now from the hell of living in ignorance of our divinity and from the self-negativity that follows from this narrow self-conception.

The Divinity of Humanity

As I have already stated, I did not see the human side of Jesus when I believed in the idealized image of him taught by conventional Christianity, but neither did I see what he revealed about my own and all humanity's identity. I have come to believe that Jesus is not the only—read *exclusive*—Son of God, but the one in whom I see that to be a human being is to be an incarnation of God. Marcus Borg states the following:

> "Son of God" is a metaphor.... It affirms that Jesus's relationship to God is intimate.... In the Hebrew Bible, Israel is called "son of God," as are the kings of Israel and Judah.[1]

The term *Son of God* is not a title indicating that Jesus's relationship with God is unique or that it sets him apart from everyone else. Rather, it is a designation that affirms what is true for every one of us: that we are the offspring of God, one with the One from whose being we are begotten. Although it may be difficult to imagine for those whose understanding and belief in Jesus continues to be shaped by traditional teachings, my current sense of who he was and is does not undo his divinity in my eyes. Affirming Jesus's humanity has made it possible for me to recognize the divinity of every person. I believe this to be the message he both taught and embodied: that each person, every last and lost one of us, incarnates the Divine.

Christianity has to do with our spiritual identity, our communion with God not as a being apart from us but as the heart of us. For many Christians, Jesus has gotten in the way of this awareness, this state of enlightenment. We have hailed him, but we have failed to see in him our own likeness to and beloved status in God. Perhaps what is needed is not to take Jesus off the pedestal but to come to the realization that there is a place on it for us as well. We share in the intimacy he shared with God, that son- or daughterhood is a way of saying we are bone of God's bone and flesh of God's flesh. After all, when his disciples asked Jesus to teach them how to pray (Luke 11:1), he didn't say pray to *my* Father, but to *our* Father; in other words, we have the capacity to share the same intimate relationship with God that he did.

I think it important to add that our oneness with God has nothing to do with piety, purity, or perfection. It is not about our behavior, but our being; not our performance, but our person. The very reality of Jesus, understood as an embodiment of God's presence in our midst, is a sacrament of the truth that God abides with us in the messiness of our humanity. When we embrace Jesus as a human being who reveals the incarnate presence of God in all beings, Christianity ceases to be identified with a code of morals or a body of beliefs and becomes instead a way of relating to both ourselves and others as precious in our brokenness.

Demoting Jesus?

While leading a discussion on the topic of Jesus's humanity with students preparing for ministry as hospital chaplains, I became aware of how heretical my understanding of Jesus may appear to those who are steeped in traditional beliefs about him. I was accused of "demoting" Jesus, of making him into someone who was essentially like everyone else. "How is he different from us?" was their question. What I heard in that query was not only a conviction having to do with the exclusivity of Jesus's divinity, but a failure to recognize the essential holiness of all humanity. I was reminded of the following passage in the gospel of Mark, where Jesus encounters his neighbors:

> He began teaching in the synagogue and most of them were astonished.... "Where did the man get all this? ... This is the carpenter, surely, the son of Mary, the brother of James and Joseph and Jude and Simon? His sisters, too, are they not with us?" And they would not accept him. (Mark 6:2–4)

It seems to me that many of Jesus's contemporaries may have rejected him because he was so much like them. How can someone from *our* neighborhood and whose family *we* know be a person of such power and importance? How can he be close to God when he is like us in so many ways?

In stating what I believe about Jesus, it is not my intention to give him a demotion but to suggest that we may have missed the message he both embodied and proclaimed: that we are one with him in God, as indicated in the following passage from John's gospel:

> May they all be one.
> Father, may they be one in us,
> As you are in me and I am in you....
> I have given them the glory you gave me,
> That they may be one as we are one.
> With me in them and you in me ...
> So that the love with which you loved me may be in
>   them,
> And so that I may be in them. (John 17:21–22, 17:26)

Jesus's Words or Words about Him?

Jesus's message was a radical—from the Latin *radix*, meaning "root"—affirmation of our underlying oneness with God. Claims to his special status in God are, scripture scholars say, less likely to be his claims than those of his followers, the community that saw in him the fulfillment of their hopes for a Messiah. Borg, for one, believes this to be true:

> A strong majority of mainline scholars think it unlikely that Jesus said these things about himself; he probably did not speak of himself as the Messiah, the Son of God, the Light of the World, and so forth. Rather, his is the voice of the community in the years and decades after Easter. It is not the language of self-proclamation, but the community's testimony to Jesus' significance in their lives.[2]

The significance of Jesus in the lives of Christians today is no less central than it was for those who first joined the movement that formed around him during his life and immediately following his death and resurrection. But I am convinced that it is possible to be a passionate Christian without believing that the statements made *about* him in the gospels were statements made *by* him. It is unlikely that he proclaimed himself to be supernatural, but he was and is Spirit-filled to those of us who are inspired by his life and his message.

I used to believe that Jesus himself said, "I am the way, the truth, and the life" (John 14:6), and that this meant that only those who believed all that he preached and all that was taught about him would be saved. Because he was the way, all other ways were a dead end. No Jew (even though Jesus was one), Hindu, Buddhist, Muslim, or other adherents of non-Christian beliefs had a snowball's chance in hell to make it to heaven. People could live what amounted to a Christian life—one characterized by loving, giving, and forgiving—but if they did not subscribe to the Christian creed, they were goners. I no longer think that belief in Jesus as "the way" means that only Christians will be saved. What I do believe is that his *way* of living aligns with the *truth* of who all people truly are (one with God) and that when we act in accord with that truth, we experience *life* to the fullest.

Jesus, when viewed through the lens of high Christology, can get in the way not only of seeing him as human and ourselves as holy but also of recognizing the relatedness of all people in God, be they Christian or non-Christian, believers or nonbelievers. While flying back to Colorado Springs one evening, I was seated next to a young woman who worked for an evangelical Christian missionary organization. She was very bright, articulate, and well-traveled. As she shared some of her missionary experiences, I was envious of the fact that she had lived in so many different cultures and that she had been exposed to such a variety of religious traditions. However, it struck me as being inconsistent with her otherwise open mind and heart when, in response to my asking whether she thought that the non-Christian peoples she had encountered would go to heaven, she replied no emphatically and without hesitation. According to a literal interpretation of the Bible, only those who have "come to Jesus" will experience eternal life.

As I see it now, the problem with the traditional understanding of Jesus as "the way" is that it isn't very Christian! A "Christians only" understanding of who will be saved is too exclusive to be in sync with the wide-open embrace with which Jesus welcomed sinners and outcasts, women and children, Samaritans and gentiles. Any understanding of the Christian faith that does not honor other belief systems is not Christian enough.

What Sets Jesus Apart

I mentioned earlier that, as human as Jesus was, I believe something extraordinary occurred in his life: his awakening to the truth that humanity is infused with divinity. Jesus seemed to experience an intimacy with God that transformed him, and he achieved a self-surrender in relation to God that set him apart from others at the same time that it drew them to him.

Jesus became what Borg calls a "God-intoxicated Jew." He was so on fire with the experience of God's pervasive and compassionate presence in himself and others that he could not remain silent when God was spoken about as distant and punitive. And when people who were suffering approached him, he could not be passive, no matter what the Jewish law taught about healing on the Sabbath. This is clear from Jesus's encounter with a man who had a withered hand: "I ask you, is it lawful to do good on the Sabbath—or evil? To preserve life—or destroy it? He looked around at them all and said to the man, 'Stretch out your hand.' The man did so and his hand was perfectly restored" (Luke 6:9–10). Jesus was a healer, a teacher, a prophet, and a reformer in ways so unconventional that he became a threat to the religious status quo and to those whose position and authority supported it.

In the same way that viewing Jesus as the one and only Son of God can prevent us from recognizing his humanity, so too can the notion that Jesus was exclusively, or even primarily, a teacher of morality get in the way of seeing him as one who challenged the conventional outlook and legalistic practices of his religious tradition. Many of the parables Jesus told have been understood as lessons in morality, instructions on how his followers should behave. But a closer look, which begins with the understanding that Jesus was impatient with both false teachings and teachers and that he was convinced of the sacredness of every person, suggests a different interpretation.

An obvious example of this is the parable of the Good Samaritan (Luke 10:29–37). In this story a priest and a Levite avoided contact with a man who was beaten and robbed, whereas a Samaritan—an outcast, according to Jewish law— treats him with compassion. This is not merely a tale about the importance of caring for all people without distinction; it is primarily an indictment of a legalistic approach to religion and those who support it. This is so because the priest and the Levite were adhering to the letter of the law by refusing to be in the vicinity of the victim, who was considered ritually unclean.

This parable and others like it reveal Jesus to be one who viewed God and religion in ways that were at odds with conventional beliefs. His was a message that invited those whom were marginalized to see themselves as fully accepted and those whom were held in high esteem to recognize the precariousness of their position.

Why Were You Not You?

Because I now see how my early understanding of Jesus has gotten in the way of realizing my own divinity, I no longer feel that I must imitate his every word and deed. However, I am convinced that if I imitate the way he was himself, if I live with the freedom that comes with an awareness of and surrender to God's indwelling, I will be "saved"; that is, I will be the person I am called to be. Jewish thinker and author Martin Buber supports this view when telling a story about Rabbi Zusya, who used to say, "In the coming world they will not ask me, 'Why were you not Moses?' They will ask me, 'Why were you not Zusya?'"[3] In other words, Why were you not the best person you could be?

It has been said that we should not seek to follow in the footsteps of the religious men and women of old, but that we ought to seek what they sought. Like the proverbial finger pointing to the moon, we must not stop short of the truth Jesus embodied and to which he pointed. Following him is the way not *to* him but *through* him to the reality of God, which was within as well as beyond him and is within as well as beyond us. I do not have to be Jesus or Moses or anyone else I admire, but if I am who I truly am—someone who is one with God—I may come to resemble those I hold in high esteem.

I am in agreement with Ralph Waldo Emerson, who said, "Is it not time to present this matter of Christianity exactly as it is, to take away all false reverence for Jesus, and not mistake the stream for the source?"[4] I believe that when we recognize Jesus as the stream and God as the source, we might also catch a glimpse of ourselves as tributaries whose lives flow from the same source that gave life to him.

Questions for Your Own Journey

How did you view Jesus when you first learned about him?

When you consider Jesus from the perspective of low Christology—that is, with an emphasis on his human attributes—does it conflict with the belief that he was or is divine? Explain.

Why or how might it be true that humanity and divinity are inseparable?

In what ways might you claim that Jesus was unique, different from anyone before or after him?

ᴑ—

5

Why Didn't Someone Tell Me I'm a Mystic?

John and Thomas give similar accounts of what Jesus taught privately ... and identify Jesus with the divine light that came into being "in the beginning." ... Yet, despite these similarities, the authors of John and Thomas take Jesus' private teachings in sharply different directions.... John ... believes that Jesus alone brings divine light to a world otherwise sunk into darkness.... Thomas expresses what would become a central theme of Jewish—and later Christian—mysticism ... that the "image of God" is hidden within everyone, although most people remain unaware of its presence.

—Elaine Pagels, *Beyond Belief*

I am a mystic, and so are you. This may seem like an outrageous claim, since in traditional religious thinking, mystics are those rare people who experience the powerful, unmediated, all-consuming presence of God. They are human, but unlike most of us, nothing gets in the way of their communing with the spirit world. By this definition, there are indeed very few mystics.

Catholic saints like John of the Cross, Teresa of Avila, and Julian of Norwich qualify. Others, like the Sufi Rumi and the Quakers George Fox and Rufus Jones, are also in the club. It is an elite group, a rare breed.

As lofty as mysticism is considered in religious circles, it is more often looked on with suspicion by others. Many equate mysticism with the occult or with New Age craziness. Others, being just a bit more kind, think mystics are navel-gazers, focused only on themselves and their own spiritual experiences. Comparative religions scholar Huston Smith sums up this cynical view when he states that in the minds of many, the word *mysticism* begins with "mist," ends in "schism," and has "I" in the middle! And spiritual teacher James Finley speaks jokingly from beneath his psychologist's hat when he claims that the difference between mystics and schizophrenics is that mystics are careful whom they talk to!

Mediocre Mystics

When I claim that we are all mystics, I do not mean that you and I belong in the company of those mentioned above. Our brand of mysticism is of a different sort—namely, mediocre. From the Latin *mediocris*, the word literally means "halfway up a mountain." We may not have attained the spiritual heights we strive for or that others have reached, but we are mystics nonetheless. This is so because mysticism is not about dwelling on the mountaintop or having peak experiences. It has to do with the astounding yet simple truth that God is the spiritual Ground of our being. No matter where we are on the climb, we are one with the One we seek. Philosophy professor and author Kerry Walters claims that historian and theologian Rufus Jones, one of the founders of the American Friends Service Committee, believed this to be true:

> For Jones ... the soul is inherently "conjunct" with God, inseparably linked with Spirit and thus by its

very nature open to the Divine. There's no need for the distracting razzmatazz of esoteric techniques and visions and ecstasies, because God is already *here*, encountered in the everyday course of life or not at all.[1]

Being only halfway up the mountain, it is easy to forget that "God is already *here*." But when we lose sight of this truth, we may fall prey to the illusion that we must strive to be "there"— at the summit, where we can experience the Divine in a flash rather than stumbling upon the sacred in the flesh.

For most of us, the summit of a face-to-face encounter with God appears to be exceedingly remote. Our lives are mostly a matter of keeping body and soul together. We do what it takes to pay the rent or mortgage, to put food on the table and gas in the car. We spend our time and energy trying to stay healthy, look presentable, and care for those in our charge. If a reporter were to follow us through our day with a video camera, recording all our activities and conversations, it would be unlikely that any of us would make the evening news. But it is right here in the midst of our not-very-newsworthy lives that engagement with God is possible. Heaven, Henry David Thoreau has said, is under our feet as well as over our head.

When I forget that both I and the ground I stand on are holy, it becomes hard for me to be present to simple tasks like preparing a meal, cleaning my house, or shopping for groceries. And it becomes difficult for me to relax: to take a leisurely walk, to spend time with a friend, or to watch a movie. I feel that instead of doing such mundane and unproductive things I should be busy saving the world or, perhaps, writing a book! I am not usually aware of why I am restless, frustrated, hard on myself, and judgmental of others. When I reflect on this, I sometimes conclude that I am unhappy because I am made for union with God, and that nothing and no one can satisfy my deepest longings. There is truth in this, but in reality it is most likely my failure to recognize God staring at me in the mirror that is the true cause of my dissatisfaction.

We are spiritual beings, but, unlike full-blown mystics past and present, we do not generally walk with an awareness of this truth. Fortunately, the reality of our communion with God is not dependent on consciousness or feeling; rather, it comes with the territory of our humanness. Whether it looks like it or not and whether we feel it or don't, we are mystics because we are a dimension of the mystery we call God; our very DNA is spiritual. Psychologist James Finley identified this truth when he wrote about the usually momentary experience of the Divine that can at times open up before us:

> In moments of meditative awakening we obscurely sense that who we are and who God is, is in some inscrutable manner one mystery. Sustained in this awareness, we realize that if we were to try to find ourselves as someone other than God, we would search in vain. If we were to search for God as other than ourselves, our search would be equally futile.... We are not God. But we are not other than God, either.[2]

This is not the self-understanding that was communicated to me through my early religious education. Although I was told that I am made in the image and likeness of God, the message I internalized was that I am first and foremost a sinner. I learned that I am a loved and forgiven sinner, but that deep down I walk this earth estranged from God, whose patience with my reluctance to repent and my lackluster attempts to attain perfection was wearing thin.

The Holiness of Humanness

I am saddened beyond words when I encounter good, sensitive, caring people who have no idea how holy they are or that they are already one with the God they are trying like hell to please. Many of the most religious people I know, those who take seriously the teachings and practices of their faith tradition, are furthest from the realization of the inseparable commingling of humanity and Divinity. This is so because conventional religion, operating on the assumption that God is a separate being, encourages contentment with pleasing or appeasing God rather than inviting believers to the shores of a higher consciousness, a self-understanding that includes God.

Some years ago, I had a dream in which I attended an air show where pilots maneuvered their planes in ways that defy gravity, logic, and common sense. As I was observing this scene, several women approached me, and one of them, commenting on the wording that adorned my sweatshirt, said, "I've never seen the words *holy* and *human* in the same sentence." I do not recall what the phrase on my sweatshirt was, but I know those words belong in the same sentence, because our humanness does not preclude holiness, and our holiness does not require us to transcend our humanity.

Christian churches talk about the dignity of the person, but there is always a *but*. We are made in God's image. Jesus died for our sins. God's mercy blankets us. *But* we had better watch our Ps and Qs. Televangelists appealing to the vulnerable, fear-ridden masses have made a very good living by stressing what pitiful creatures we are and how hopeless our plight is unless we manage to change our sinful ways—which they are more than happy to help with for a "small" donation.

While watching television one evening, I recall seeing a program made up of video clips from some of Billy Graham's crusades. Graham is something of an icon; he is a legend in the annals of American religion. He stands above the Jimmy Swaggarts, Jim Bakkers, and other prime-time preachers who have given a bad name to their profession. But even so, I was struck by the tenor of Graham's message. For a good fifteen minutes, the focus of his sermon was on the sorry state of our humanity, the sin-riddled reality of our lives. Only in the final few minutes did he refer to the fact of God's mercy and love for us, and never once was there a hint of the divine dimension of human nature.

Becoming Who We Are

I am not blind to the reality of our imperfection. I am not claiming that we do not need to grow beyond the selfishness, pettiness, pride, and greed that too often characterize our relationships. But what is needed more than anything is for us to *become who we are*. We are mediocre mystics. We are people whose souls are one with the universal Soul. We are, beneath all that appears contrary to it, dimensions of the Divine. Thomas Merton knew this to be true and gave expression to it when he wrote:

> There is only one problem on which all my exis-
> tence, my peace and my happiness depend: to dis-
> cover myself in discovering God. If I find Him I will
> find myself and if I find my true self I will find Him.[3]

Merton himself was a mediocre mystic. He became a monk after spending much of his adolescence and early adulthood chasing wine and women. He did not leave his humanity at the gate when he entered monastic life, but he continued to struggle with his ego-based needs and fears until his death, a fact that he documents in detail in his journals. Despite his struggles, or perhaps because of them, he became a profoundly spiritual man who experienced intimacy with God both in soli- tude and in solidarity with others. Much of his popularity and power as a spiritual mentor stems from the fact that he became more human at the same time that he became more holy.

Only when I became acquainted with the life and writings of Merton was I able to move beyond the idea that holiness and humanness are antithetical. The message Merton conveys, which is at the heart of all contemplative spirituality, posits the incarnate nature of Divinity, the mind-boggling and heart- warming good news of our goodness because of our God-ness.

There is a Buddhist saying that claims "There is nowhere to go, nothing to attain, no one to become." Why go anywhere when what we long to be in communion with is one with us right where we are? What can we possibly attain that will bring us more than the "all" that we already possess? If true happiness requires being in touch with the Spirit that is present in all people, ourselves included, how can becoming someone else be any more satisfying than being the spiritual beings we already are? The circumstances of our lives may be far from ideal, but the sacred reality with which they are infused is as pervasively present as the air we breathe. When we become aware of this truth, we can say with the mystic Julian of Norwich that "all is well" even when in the daily round of our bodily existence, all is not well.

All was not well in Paula's life when she had a dream she shared with me in a spiritual direction session. In the dream Paula was standing in front of a mirror admiring a simple but elegant dress she had just purchased. She was pleased with the dress and with how she looked wearing it. She attempted to put on a belt and some jewelry, but they fell to the floor. Upon waking she had a strong intuition that the dress was a symbol of her soul. She realized that there was a dimension of her self that was simple, elegant, and not in need of adornment. She knew instinctively that if she claimed that soul-self as her true identity, she would be at peace with herself, with others, and with life. Within a week of having this dream, Paula had several encounters with people who would have triggered a very different and less gentle response from her had she not begun to embrace her soul.

When, like a stone skipping across the surface of a pond, we move through life unaware of the divine depths within, we tend to judge people and situations according to our likes and dislikes. If someone or something gives us pleasure, we are happy, content, or grateful—all is well. When the opposite occurs, when life is not the bowl of cherries we prefer, we are likely to be displeased and ungrateful—all is not well. But when we plunge beneath the surface and become attuned to our soul-self, we tend not to be judgmental; we become better able to live with a sense of well-being, even in the midst of trials and tribulations. It is amazing to be in the presence of people who, in the face of illness, death, divorce, failure, and the like, are able to meet life's difficult times with a quiet gracefulness.

In her book *Beyond Belief*, church historian Elaine Pagels states that Gnostic Christians, many of whom were the mystics of the early church, experienced the presence of Christ and the nearness of God both within and around themselves. For a variety of less than lofty reasons, mystics became suspect, and those who were considered such were marginalized and labeled heretics. But mysticism has survived, and the truth it posits remains a reality not just for Jesus or for those recognized or canonized as mystics by the church, as Pagels states:

> God's light shines not only in Jesus but, potentially
> at least, in everyone. Thomas's gospel encourages the
> hearer not so much to *believe in Jesus* ... as to *seek to
> know* God through one's own divinely given capacity,
> since all are created in the image of God.[4]

Why didn't someone tell me this? Why don't those who have the position and authority to do so proclaim from the pulpit and the rooftops that all people—every last one of us, no matter how battered—are mystics? I suppose the simple answer is that you can't preach or teach what you don't know. Most abusers have been abused. Most of those who fail to communicate the godliness of our person are themselves victims of a negative self-understanding, or at least one that is devoid of divinity. But no matter what the reason, the reality is that most of us never learned the full extent of our identity—namely, that we are one with the One with whom we long to be one.

Encountering Our Shadow

It can be hard to imagine that we are mystics when our introspection reveals darkness rather than light, confusion rather than clarity, a mess rather than a sacred mystery. If we are an incarnation of God, should not the opposite be evident? The spiritual path that leads to the discovery of our interior union with God meanders through a murky mess. Those aspects of ourselves of which we are not proud and that we try to keep hidden from sight lurk just beneath the surface of our personas. When we stop, when we allow ourselves to be alone, when we muster the courage to take an honest look at who we are, we come face-to-face with the shadowy self described by C. S. Lewis as a "zoo of lusts, a bedlam of ambitions, a nursery of fears, a harem of fondled hatreds."[5]

How can anyone filled with the likes of these monsters be even a mediocre mystic? Annie Dillard writes about the journey through darkness to light:

> In the deeps are the violence and terror of which psychology has warned us. But if you ride these monsters down, if you drop with them farther over the world's rim, you find what our sciences cannot locate or name, the substrate, the ocean, or matrix or ether which buoys the rest ... our complex and inexplicable caring for each other, and for our life together here.[6]

A few weeks before the release of the film based on her book *Dead Man Walking*, I saw Sister Helen Prejean interviewed on a television talk show. When asked why she worked with death-row prisoners, she replied, "Because everyone is always more than the worst thing they've ever done." We are more than the worst aspects of ourselves. Beneath the darkness there is light. Before we are the complex, self-defeating, anything-but-holy people we may have become in our actions and relationships, we are one with God: spiritual beings, mediocre mystics who need to wake up to the wonder of ourselves as the locus of the Divine.

It is the embrace of the inner darkness, not its exclusion, that gives birth to the peace of mind and heart that characterizes mystics. It is brokenness humbly accepted, not perfection, that makes room for God. I have discovered that it is better to embrace myself as one who is imperfect than it is to demand perfection as a criterion for self-acceptance. It is second nature for everyone I know to strive for perfection. When we identify a fault, a shortcoming, or an aspect of our character that is problematic, many of us instinctively attempt to root it out so that we can be the person we want to be, one who resembles the ideal presented to us by family, church, and society in general. But this striving doesn't usually result in achieving our goal. Rather, it ends in frustration as we remain the flawed person we have always been.

Life will be a battleground until we become wise enough to make peace with ourselves—flaws and all. This does not preclude attentiveness to our faults. Self-compassion is a radical acceptance of our goodness despite our imperfections. In religious language, this is a willingness to surrender to God, whose love for us is unconditional. All our attempts to change for the better will be short-lived unless they begin with this truth, for we soon tire of the task when our goal is to be rid of our imperfections. The humble embrace of the crack, the flaw, and the imperfection allows Divinity's light to both get in and shine forth from us as compassion.

While I was speaking about this with a group focusing on spiritual concerns, an objection was raised concerning the possibility that accepting our faults could lead to resignation, to giving up on changing what may be both self-defeating and hurtful to others. It is important to distinguish between accepting our faults and accepting ourselves as people who have faults; spiritual maturity is a matter of the latter. If we truly desire to grow, if we open ourselves to the honest feedback of those we trust, and if we are compassionate toward ourselves, it is not likely that we will settle for being less than our best. Instead, we will stay on the high road that leads to our full development as whole and holy people.

Mystics Are Lovers

Along with the ability to befriend the inner darkness, another characteristic of mystics, mediocre or otherwise, is that they are smitten: they are in love with God, with people, with life, with something or someone as well as with themselves. With this passion comes a dying to self-preoccupation and the freedom to become one with whatever the present moment holds. It is this freedom and wholehearted entry of life that distinguishes mystics like Meister Eckhart and Teresa of Avila from many of those whose sense of self and of God is entirely separate. The latter are good, religious people who fear God, care for others, are sincere believers, and participate in the various rituals and devotions of their faith tradition, but they often lack a joie de vivre. They have not been swept off their feet. The boundary that separates them from all that is not them has not been broken, as it was for Rumi. Roger Housden writes about how Rumi's world was turned upside down in the face of love:

> Rumi had lived a life of serious study and ascetic prac-
> tice before he even met Shams of Tabiz, the man who
> was to set his heart on fire.... Rumi was an exemplary
> teacher ... a truly good man. But he had not known
> love. Love shook him to the foundations. It made him
> a madman in the eyes of some of his followers.[7]

"He was a serious student." "She was deeply ascetic." "He was an exemplary teacher." "She was a truly good person." If these words were engraved on our tombstones, they would indicate that our lives were well lived. But if it could not be said of us that we were madly in love with life, perhaps we were not so alive after all.

The capacity to be undone by love is an aspect of mystics that makes them the best communicators of the word of God. Fritz, a long time friend, once told me that he learned this while facilitating a discussion with a group of ministers. The participants, who were from all over the world, were spending six months in a sabbatical program, after which they would return to their various work assignments. On this occasion, the group was discussing what it took to be a good preacher. One person thought the most important quality of a preacher was her or his willingness to spend long hours in prayer. Another believed that immersion in the scriptures was most essential. Still another thought that the appropriate use of metaphor and humor was first and foremost. Finally, a woman from an African country stood up and said, "Good preachers are people who are in love. I don't care whether they are in love with a man, a woman, or a dog; they just have to be in love."

Passionate preaching is a by-product of a love affair with God, known and experienced as one with us in our relationship with ourselves, with others, and with the world. The bottom line of all this mystical business is not that we are able to experience brief or prolonged moments of spiritual ecstasy but that we are human enough to love and be loved. This is so because mysticism is about our communion with the Divine, and Divinity, the Christian tradition proclaims, is love incarnate in us and as us.

Questions for Your Own Journey

Why, despite the radical sound of it, might you say with confidence that you too are a mystic?

Identify a time in your life when you experienced what Julian of Norwich described as "all is well," despite the outward fact that it was not.

Who, if anyone, related to you in such a way that you felt special to, exceptional to, loved by, or close to God?

What aspects of your self do you encounter when you look within?

6

Inspiration Is Not Dictation

Just as this view of the Bible [historical and meta-phorical] does not deny the reality of God, it does not deny that the Bible is "inspired by God." But it understands inspiration differently.... Inspiration refers to the movement of the Spirit in the lives of the people who produced the Bible. The emphasis is not upon *words* inspired by God, but on *people* moved by their experience of the Spirit.
   —Marcus Borg, *The Heart of Christianity*

It may have been apparent in the Introduction to this book that I believe Annie Dillard knows a thing or two about walking the "spiritual path." I also believe she has a good grasp of the notion of inspiration, or she could not have written these words:

Something pummels us, something barely sheathed. Power broods and lights. We are played on like a pipe; our breath is not our own.[1]

To be inspired is to be enlivened by the Spirit. It is to be moved in such a way that thoughts, words, and actions come *through* us more than they come *from* us.

So it was for those who authored the books that make up the Bible and, I believe, those who composed noncanonical writings like the gospels of Thomas, Philip, Judas, and Mary. They were "played on like a pipe"; they were instruments through which the music of sacred stories was played. But, like us, they were human instruments, people whose experiences and beliefs affected what came through them.

When I first became acquainted with the Bible, it did not occur to me to question the historical accuracy of its stories or its worldview. These were givens that met my need for certitude and for a sense of God's guiding presence. Because the Bible was "true," I knew what to believe and how to live so as to please God.

Although the Bible took second place to sacraments in the pre–Vatican II Catholicism in which I was raised, there was nonetheless a reverence for it and an assumption—except in scholarly circles—of its utter truth. The Bible's many books, both in the Hebrew Bible and Christian Scriptures, were, along with tradition, church teachings, and revelation, the source and sum of what I needed to know about all things religious.

Inspiration Is Passionate Communication

I didn't realize it at the time, but the literal approach to scripture on which I was weaned and that influenced my life for decades was limiting rather than liberating, because it failed to distinguish between inspiration and dictation. The purpose and value of inspirational writing lies not in its being an accurate recounting of what one has been told, but in the passionate communication of what one experiences as true. Inspiration allows for fantasy and fiction, embellishment and exaggeration, whereas dictation is a matter of accuracy, first and foremost.

When I was told as a child that the Bible was inspired writing, I, like so many others, concluded that this meant God had dictated every word to the authors of its various books and that it was to be accepted without question as historically factual. But I have now come to see that this perspective is too simplistic. It creates an adversarial relationship between religion and logic, between scripture and science.

Many who claim that the Bible is factually accurate reject the findings of scripture scholars, historians, archaeologists, and others whose research challenges a literal interpretation of many biblical stories. Examples include the creation story (Genesis 1:1–31), the account of Adam and Eve in the Garden of Eden (Genesis 3:1–24), and the infancy narratives (Luke 2:1–20). Reliable biblical scholarship has shown that many influences were at work in the formation of these and other biblical texts and that they are more the product of a faith community's beliefs than the direct hand of God. Christian theologian Marcus Borg writes in support of this view:

> The Bible is the historical product of two ancient communities, ancient Israel and the early Christian movement. The Bible was not written to us or for us, but for the ancient communities that produced it.
> ... As such, it is a human product, not a divine product. This claim in no way denies the reality of God. Rather, it sees the Bible as the response of these ancient communities to God.[7]

To say that the Bible is not a divine product may not deny the reality of God, but it does seem to undermine its significance. For millennia Christians have lived their lives based on the understanding that the Bible comes directly from God, and many have given their lives for the values it espouses. I have immense respect for those whose belief that the Bible was "written" by God has moved them to live with generosity and compassion; the "Good Book" has inspired millions of people to live very good lives.

The Problem with Dictation

But it is also true that the Bible and the scriptures of other faith traditions, when read literally, have given birth to ways of thinking and acting that are contrary to the values of good religion and inconsistent with a good God. When the Bible is believed to be dictated by God, all kinds of madness follows: creationists do battle over how life began with those who stand on the firm ground of evolution; expeditions venture forth to find the ruins of Noah's Ark; Jehovah's Witnesses, among others, refuse to allow the transfusion of blood or blood products, based on their literal understanding of the seventeenth chapter of the book of Leviticus and 1 Samuel 14:32–33; and predictions about the end of the world come and go, based on calculations from the book of Revelation. Everything from war to dietary restrictions to the condemnation of homosexuals has biblical confirmation for those who think that inspiration is synonymous with dictation.

We must be discerning in the way we read the Bible and in how we apply it to life. Its significance is undermined not because it is a human product but because by misinterpreting its meaning, we can become unreasonable in our worldview and unloving in our attitudes and actions.

What distinguishes those who confuse inspiration with dictation from those who do not is whether the human element operative in the creation of scripture is taken into account. On his website, Bishop John Shelby Spong states the following in response to a question concerning the Bible's origin:

> The Bible was written between 1000 BCE and 135 CE. It has in it transcendent and inspired insights but it also has in it tribal prejudices, ancient ignorance, and a pre-modern worldview.... God does not endorse slavery or war or the second-class status for women or the execution of gay people. Yet the Bible attributes all of these things to God.

> The Bible is a human book written by human
> beings who were trying to understand who they are
> and who God is.[3]

The Bible is a complex compendium of books whose authors were real people who were influenced by the times in which they lived. Chroniclers of their culture's religious history, they recorded experiences and stories that had been told verbally for generations. Who were the authors of scripture? Who were their mentors? When and where did they live? What was happening socially, politically, and religiously at the time they wrote? These questions and others like them weigh heavily on what these people believed and communicated. Although it may be easier to ignore such questions, these influences must be taken into account in order to decipher the accuracy of their message.

Those of us who distinguish between inspiration and dictation do not question the truth of biblical accounts chronicling God's involvement in the lives of the Hebrew people and the early followers of Jesus, but we seek to discern the influence of the historical context on what those accounts convey.

I believe it is human nature to be drawn toward the literal, not only with regard to scripture but in other aspects of life as well. It is comforting to look at life without nuance; it is simpler that way—easier to understand and less confusing when it comes to making decisions. But whether it's the letter of the law or the letters (words) of the Bible, when we interpret them literally we run the risk of missing what gives them meaning and what in their message can give meaning to our lives. Philosopher Sam Keen writes about this truth, "Literalism concentrates on the letter and misses the spirit; it gets the words but never the music.... You can starve to death trying to eat a cookbook."[4]

Ingesting the Bible, knowing it chapter and verse, can't nourish our souls any more than eating a cookbook can nourish our bodies. If we want to be true to its music, we must not be content with ingesting the Bible, we must digest it as well. We must allow its stories to warm our hearts, its lessons to inform our actions, and its meaning to permeate our being. When this happens, we come to embody the truth the Bible conveys: the compassionate presence of God is in our midst.

Scripture As Myth and Metaphor

Many people believe that scripture is too sacred to mess with. But I believe that it is *so* sacred that we must mess with it; that is, we must do everything possible to discern its historical, spiritual, and religious meaning by means of faith-filled, rigorous scholarship. A man of faith and integrity, German theologian and scripture scholar Rudolph Bultmann is associated with the form of biblical criticism called "demythologizing." Demythologizing attempts to discern what is factual from what is mythical in biblical writings in order to correctly interpret mythological statements. This approach to scripture was a turning point in my life, for it moved me beyond literal thinking and opened me to a broader and more liberating understanding of these sacred writings.

A critical approach to reading the Bible opened my eyes to the fact that it need not be factually correct for it to be a vehicle of the truth. The Bible is awash with wonderful stories about events that may never have happened and outrageous characters of whom many may never have existed. And yet, through the telling of its tales, the great lessons of life and of God's involvement in human history have become rooted in our psyches.

Buried within the stories that make up the Bible is a treasure trove of archetypal truths that offer us a way of understanding and relating to God, life, and ourselves that is empowering. God's creative spirit breathes in us. All humanity is a chosen people. God's love is a covenant we can count on. We will, if we trust God, be led out of bondage to freedom. When we open ourselves to the Spirit within, not even death can extinguish the light and life that is our true, God-infused self. These truths are dynamic, hopeful, and filled with a vitality that can see us through the darkest corners of life with courage and confidence.

When I was a child, the four words I most wanted to hear were *once upon a time*. This phrase signaled the beginning of stories that were both fictional and fanciful. Tales like "Hansel and Gretel," "Cinderella," and "Jack and the Beanstalk" cast a spell, created an aura, and told a truth about the sometimes precarious adventure we call life. These stories carried me into a world that seemed to be more real than the one in which I lived.

But as I grew older and, I thought, wiser, I began to discount the stories that permeated my childhood; I viewed them as childish compared to *real* stories about *real* people in the *real* world. But thanks to my exposure to good scripture scholarship and to the writings of Joseph Campbell and Carl Jung, I have now come to realize that story, myth, and metaphor are the way to convey the most important truths.

Myths are not fables. They are eternal stories that are forever true not in their detail but in their message and meaning. Writing about this, Marcus Borg states:

> I have been told that German novelist Thomas Mann defined myth ... as "a story about the way things never were, but always are." So, is a myth true? Literally true, no. Really true, yes.[5]

Also writing about the power of mythical stories, Roger Housden says:

> Stories are what make us ... not the other way around.... Stories feed the imagination, which is our connection between who we are and who we may be, between our individual existence and the bigger stories of the race and the culture ... between our own tiny ship of a soul and the vastness of the ocean on which we sail.[6]

An appreciation of the mythic nature of biblical stories can enable us to recognize and perhaps be consoled by the fact that the twists and turns of our individual lives are part of the human story that has been experienced and retold throughout history.

Among biblical myths is the story of the Exodus, which illustrates that all of life is a series of leave-takings from the Egypt of our confinement (relationships, places, beliefs), and the story of our subsequent wandering before coming to the Promised Land of dreams fulfilled—a "place" that may itself become confining in time. Other biblical myths include Jonah's three-day stay in the belly of a whale, which can be read as a prototype of Jesus's entombment as well as the story of humanity's reluctance to heed God's call and the consequences we pay for our unwillingness to do so. And there are the infancy narratives and the myth of the virgin birth, which proclaim not only with what reverence the early Christian community held Jesus but how, like Mary, we are called to give birth to the Christ (the holy in us) by entrusting ourselves to the power of God.

Scripture's Stories Are Our Stories

Myth is a powerful and engaging way to tell the truth not only about the heroes and heroines who are the main characters in the stories but about ourselves as well. When I began to think of biblical figures as mythical, it made it easier for me to see their story as *our* story. Although David was, in fact, a person who actually lived, in the story about his confrontation with Goliath (1 Samuel 17:48–49), he is mythical, as is the giant of a man he is said to have slain. The truth of that story and of those characters is repeated daily as the weak take on the strong, both individually and institutionally. When the underdog wins the contest, when the poor laborers organize to strike for better working conditions, it is David and Goliath all over again. As an example of this, I think of César Chavez, who, in the 1960s and 1970s, led migrant farmworkers in their quest for better working conditions and a just wage.

Viewing biblical stories from a mythical perspective can make them come alive with a relevance that gives hope, courage, and meaning as we move through the years and the fears that are our life stories. A biblical myth that has meaning for me personally is the story about the Israelites making a golden calf as their impatience got the best of them while awaiting Moses's return from his rendezvous with Yahweh (Exodus 32:1–6). Time and again I grow weary waiting for Moses—that is, waiting for a sign, a message, a guide in the desert of my uncertainty. And I worship "golden calves" in the form of projects, people, and my own body as a way of distracting myself from my true longing for God.

The addictions that afflict many of us as we meander through life are false gods that we worship in order to fill an inner void, an emptiness that, if we embraced it, could make way for the Presence for which we long. A subtle example of a void-filling false god is the busyness with which many of us occupy ourselves so as not to be alone with our thoughts and feelings. People in our culture will do almost anything to avoid the void of being still, silent, and alone. We seek meaning and a sense of purpose through relationships and productivity, both of which are good, but we often fail to experience the value of ourselves independent of people and supercharged activity.

Within the mythical meaning of scripture's stories are the many metaphors that can help us understand the particular circumstances of our lives in relation to a larger truth, as Joseph Campbell states:

> Spiritual truths that transcend time and space can only be borne in metaphorical vessels whose meaning is found in their connotations.... Religious metaphors are rich, [are] timeless, and refer not to somebody else in the outer world of another era but to us and our inner spiritual existence right now.[7]

A metaphor is a word or an image that stands for or represents a larger truth. The parting of the Red Sea is a metaphor within the Exodus myth that speaks of the against-all-odds passage to freedom that each of us is called to take from time to time. The cross and the empty tomb are other metaphors that represent the need to die to what is false in us and the new life that issues from this death. When we recognize the metaphorical elements of the Bible, it becomes more than the story of our religious ancestors. Instead, it becomes the ageless account of humanity's journey with and to God.

Now that I have an appreciation for the power of myth and metaphor, I would say that scripture should be *remythologized*. It is still important to distinguish between what is factual and what is not, but it is even more important to appreciate and embrace the Bible's sometimes outlandish stories that shed light on life as we live it. To remythologize scripture is to honor the nonliteral, storylike manner with which religious truths were conveyed at a time and in a culture that was less concerned about facts and more focused on the larger-than-life reality of God's workings in the world.

The Bible is sacred writing not because God dictated its every word, but because it conveys through myth and metaphor the Spirit that inspired those who authored it. If the scriptures of all faith traditions were understood to be vessels of mythical truth, they could become a source of connection across religious boundaries, since their wisdom is universal. But when they are embraced with a fundamentalist mind-set and are thought to be the one and only expression of God's word and will, scriptures can, and tragically have, become the cause of division and bloodshed in the name of God.

Questions for Your Own Journey

Presuming that you have been inspired, describe how it felt and what it led you to do.

When you first encountered the Bible, what did you learn about its authority?

In what ways has the Bible shaped your life? How has its message made you a better person?

In what biblical stories and parables can you see yourself?

7

Morality As Right Relationship

Morality is a redemptive process. In the light of God's revelation in Jesus Christ, human life is not a purely natural reality. Human life is always supernatural. God is redemptively present in the process by which man becomes more truly human.... God is present to man in the faith, hope, and love which are the basis of all moral life.

—Gregory Baum, *Man Becoming*

What a novel thought it is that "human life is always supernatural" and that morality has to do with becoming "more truly human." If, like me, you think this is odd, perhaps it is because you were taught what I was taught: that being human is merely natural not supernatural, and that morality is the process not of becoming more truly human, but of keeping our human nature in check. In his book *The Wisdom of Wilderness*, psychiatrist Gerald May makes this point by describing a scene from the motion picture *The African Queen*:

Charlie Allnut (Humphrey Bogart), having had a bit too much to drink the night before, awakens to find Rose Sayer (Katharine Hepburn) pouring his bottles of gin into the Zambezi River.

"Whatcha bein' so mean for, Miss?" he pleads. "A man takes a drop too much once in a while, it's ... it's only human nature."

"Nature, Mr. Allnut," she replies, "is what we are put in this world to rise above."[1]

Rose Sayer sounds a lot like the priests and nuns who formed my thinking about moral matters. Like her, they operated on the assumption that human nature is "fallen"—that we have lost any innocence we might have had—and that we are now prone to sin and in need of constant vigilance and discipline lest we succumb to it. This perspective was reinforced for me by the *Baltimore Catechism*, which states, "On account of the sin of Adam, we, his descendants, come into the world deprived of sanctifying grace and inherit his punishment."[2]

Because none of us are innocent and all of us are prone to sin, moral directives are essential guides as we negotiate the spiritual path. However, their often negative "Thou shalt not" formulation feels unnecessarily rigid and frigid to me because such language lacks the flexibility and warmth that ought to characterize anything having to do with God. Journalist and social critic H. L. Mencken's cynical definition of morality is not far from what I was taught: "Morality is the theory that every human act must be either right or wrong, and that 99 percent of them [sic] are wrong."[3]

Given that Mencken's definition of morality resonated with me, it should be no surprise that my earliest motivation for doing good and avoiding evil was primarily the consequences of my actions. What will happen to me in this life and the next if I do something that's considered wrong? And what's in it for me if I do the right thing? It was all about fear of punishment and hope for reward, which, according to psychologist Lawrence

Kohlberg's study of moral development, are the earliest and least mature stages.

Heavy-Handed Morality

The moral air I breathed as a child created in me a sense of anxiety, the ingredients of which were fear and guilt. When a discomforting intuition alerts us to the fact that we are not being true to ourselves, guilt is good. But most religious guilt is the product of neurotic fears that emphasize our imperfection and God's presumed wrath. Like the bumper sticker that reads "I saw that. God," I was given the impression that when it comes to seeing our misdeeds, God has 20/20 vision. This way of thinking has kept some of us from attaining spiritual maturity but has, for countless others, been emotionally crippling.

I feel both sad and angry when I think about some of the people I have counseled in psychiatric units in hospitals where I've worked, for in most cases their emotional burdens were either caused or worsened by their fear of a vengeful God. This was the case with Sam, a forty-nine-year-old man who was diagnosed with a form of obsessive-compulsive disorder. Sam could not let go of the thoughts that continually found him guilty for the sexual fantasies and actions (masturbation) that dominated his adolescent years. His compulsive hand-washing was a ritual attempt to alleviate his guilt. As we spoke, it became clear that the condemning voice Sam had internalized was that of the minister at the church of his youth, a man who preached hellfire and brimstone sermons that were often focused on the evils of sex. Sexuality, especially in adolescence, is a minefield for most of us, but add the threatening messages often communicated by religious authorities, and it is unlikely that anyone would survive that precarious developmental phase free of psychosexual hangups.

It has been said that heavy-handed morality in a household where a parent or another adult is quick to accuse, judge, and condemn in the name of God results in the same kind of dysfunction as growing up in an alcoholic family. Fear, uncertainty, the sense of walking on eggs, denial of feelings, secret keeping, and the like ensue, and they create unhealthy family dynamics and stunted individual development.

Some people were fortunate not to have lived under that oppressive cloud at home but, like Sam, experienced the same thing in parochial schools or within a church community. This was the case in my own life. My family was more functional than most; never once do I recall the fear of God being used to keep me in line. But the formal religious education I received in a Catholic school and the air I breathed at the church where my family worshipped had a decidedly negative bent. The emphasis of moral teachings was on avoiding sin and its "near occasion" and on the punishment that awaited me if I failed to do so.

When the tyrannical voice of moral righteousness rules a family or a classroom, or when the word of God is preached with unbending harshness from the pulpit, what is communicated is that our worth as people and our acceptability in the eyes of God depend on our compliance with particular norms of behavior. Whether intended or not, the message is that we are not loved or lovable until we get it right.

Abiding by Rules or Abiding in God

In grappling with the negative notion of morality, I have tried to recognize and rescue the baby in the bathwater—that is, to embrace the importance of moral parameters without ceding power to the guilt and fear associated with them. This endeavor has made me realize that morality is essentially about right relationship rather than appropriate behavior. It is more about abiding in God than abiding by rules. Living a moral life is not merely a matter of obeying religious laws, but of recognizing in them the articulation of a higher directive (love) that is written on our hearts. Jesuit priest William Johnston echoes this notion when he writes:

And this, I maintain, is the very apex of Christian morality. No longer fidelity to law but submission to the guidance of love."[4]

My reading of the gospels leads me to believe that Jesus knew that abiding in God was more important than abiding by rules. Many Christians tend to see Jesus as having been a good Jew, which he was. He was familiar with the Torah, he attended synagogue services, he gave alms, and he tended to the less fortunate. But what often fails to register with us is that he broke as many religious rules as he kept. He healed on the Sabbath, befriended sinners, welcomed women as close disciples, and challenged the righteousness of religious authority figures. In this he did not thumb his nose at the rules and rituals of Judaism, but he demonstrated what it meant to be a truly good Jew—namely, to be faithful to the inner promptings of the Spirit even when doing so put him at odds with conventional religious morality.

There are times and circumstances in which breaking the letter of the law is the right thing to do. I believe that naturalist John James Audubon may have had this idea in mind when he said, "When the bird and the book disagree, always believe the bird." When the voice of conscience is at odds with the law of the land, the church, or any other authority, we must believe and act in accordance with the voice. In one example of conscience trumping law, friends of mine were arrested for trespassing at an air force base while protesting the U.S. participation in space weaponry development. They were obviously in violation of civil law (the book), but their actions were in keeping with the Spirit (the bird) that called them to stand up against anything that could cause harm to any human being.

In Harmony with the Tao

My belief that morality has to do with right relationship has been influenced by Taoism, an ancient philosophical and religious tradition of Chinese origin. It developed in part in response to Confucianism, which, like most religions of the West, stressed the primacy of virtue: it is by right actions that we become good. The Taoist philosopher Chuang Tzu (369–286 BCE) taught that being attuned to the Tao (Way), not virtuousness, was the essence of goodness. Being at one with the guiding principle of life, the simple good underlying all things, the order beneath chaos, is the way to a fulfilling life individually and an ordered life collectively. In the introduction to his work on Taoism, Thomas Merton states the following:

> For Chuang Tzu, the truly great man is therefore not the man who has, by a lifetime of study and practice, accumulated a great fund of virtue and merit, but the man in whom "Tao acts without impediment."[5]

Being a person in whom Tao or God acts without impediment does not minimize the importance of traditional morality, for without an objective reference point, our moral compass can easily take us off course. The term *following our conscience* can be a euphemism for doing whatever we want. A relational understanding of morality changes the emphasis from compliance to congruence, from striving to be good to resting in God, from keeping rules to growing toward a harmonious union with the Sacred both within and beyond our selves.

This same emphasis can also be found in Western religions. Terms like *union of wills*, *purity of heart*, and *dying to self* so common in the lexicon of Christianity refer to a relationship with God in which no trace of the ego or false self is to be found. Through meditation and other spiritual practices, we are invited to undergo a transformation that closes the gap between God and our soul. In fact, there is no gap, only a lack of awareness of our oneness with God. But the failure to realize the truth of this union has resulted in a kind of busy morality characterized by the pursuit of virtue rather than a more contemplative, mystical communing with God.

Because I was taught that being virtuous was synonymous with being moral, I find it nothing less than revolutionary to think that morality has less to do with the attainment of virtue than with being in union with God. But as I reflect on the unfolding of my life, I can see the wisdom of this teaching. My experience is that morality, understood as striving for virtue, has served only to focus attention on myself. When my attempts to be virtuous succeed, I am uplifted. When they fail, I am deflated. It's all about me. But when my focus is on being in sync with Tao, God, or Spirit—the essence of which is love—I tend to forget myself and live, instead, with a higher consciousness and a freer spirit. I have also found that the virtue I once strove to attain has now begun to manifest itself independent of my efforts—true morality is more about grace than willpower, more about God than it is about us.

Free from Self, Free for Others

When we abide in God and live attuned to the Spirit, we become liberated from self-preoccupation with its focus on sin, repentance, sacrifice, and the like. Our attention shifts from concern only about the state of our souls before God to one that includes the "state of the union," the condition of the world and the quality of our relationships with others—especially those in greatest need.

In my role as a confessor, I noticed that most of the people who presented themselves for the Sacrament of Reconciliation (confession) did so with the consciousness that they had sinned and that they must repent in order to be in God's good graces. In the meeting of penitent and confessor, it is common to hear someone say, "Bless me, Father, for I have sinned. I lied, I cheated, I had impure thoughts, and I got angry with my neighbor." But it is rare to hear, "I remained passively silent when I could have come to the aid of a falsely accused coworker" or "I failed to give my time and energy to the cause of the homeless and hungry in my community."

Although I believe with St. Paul that "nothing can separate us from the love of God" (Romans 8:39), the need for repentance, for a change of heart, can be appropriate, for despite our best efforts, we all stand in need of forgiveness for offenses of omission and commission. It is also true that in a broader understanding of sin, we are responsible for the general brokenness, the less-than-healthy condition of humanity in which we participate and to which we contribute by our selfishness, greed, judgmental attitudes, and the like. But moral people, while being appropriately concerned with their own faults, do not overlook their responsibility to and for the world.

The Moral of Our Story

Another way to think about the important notion of morality has to do with learning the deepest truths about ourselves: who we are and how we are to live. When a story conveys a truth about life, we say it has a moral. This is the case with Greek myths, Aesop's fables, and Jesus's parables, to name just a few examples. Perhaps morality can be looked at in this way, rather than being thought of only as religious prescriptions having to do with right and wrong behavior. Life's unfolding is a story full of lessons to be learned, truths to internalize and apply to our endeavors and relationships. As we integrate and live what we learn, we grow in moral maturity.

The moral of our lives is revealed when we open ourselves to the shadow and light within as well as to all that we encounter in life. Our strengths and weaknesses, altruism and selfishness, faith and fears, successes and failures, loves and losses, and joys and sorrows can bring us to the humbling awareness that despite our folly, we are the locus of the divine. Thomas Merton, speaking with full awareness of the poverty of his attempts to achieve holiness, once expressed this truth in a journal entry:

> I am noisy, full of the racket of my imperfections and passions, and the wide open wounds left by my sins.

Full of my own emptiness. Yet, ruined as my house
is, You live there!⁶

That God lives in us even when we are at our worst can be a
transforming realization. To embrace this truth, instead of
dwelling on the "wide open wounds left by [our] sins," can
enable us to pick up the broken pieces of our lives and move
forward in faith. This movement, this sometimes awkward stag-
gering toward and with God, is the spiritual journey wherein we
discover the moral and meaning of our lives.

Like the mythological heroes whose journeys to greatness
took them through trying circumstances, we often learn the
moral of our life stories through experiences that are difficult, if
not devastating. Author and educator Parker Palmer writes about
learning the moral of his life through a bout with depression:

> After hours of careful listening, my therapist offered
> an image that helped me eventually reclaim my life.
> "You seem to look upon depression as the hand of an
> enemy trying to crush you," he said. "Do you think
> you could see it instead as the hand of a friend, press-
> ing you down to ground on which it is safe to stand?"
>
> ... I developed my own image of the "befriending"
> impulse behind my depression. Imagine that from
> early in my life, a friendly figure ... was trying to get
> my attention....
>
> The figure calling to me all those years was, I
> believe, what Thomas Merton calls "true self." This
> is not the ego self.... It is the self planted in us by
> God who made us in God's own image—the self that
> wants nothing more or less than for us to be who we
> were created to be.⁷

When I read Palmer's account of his struggle to find the person
he was created to be, I was reminded of my own attempt to
discover the moral of my story and my life path. I had been a

Catholic priest in a religious order for thirty-two years, but as the years passed, I began feeling less than alive in that life. Like Palmer, I had been striving to be who I thought I wanted to be and who I thought I should be, but in doing so I was not accepting who I truly am: someone who needs to be grounded in a significant relationship. I have learned that, for me, this is the ground on which it is safe to stand. It is not ground with greener grass but the ground on which I have discovered that God and the ground of my soul are one and the same. For when we love and are loved in all aspects of our being, the notion that "God is love" becomes the experience that love is God incarnate.

In one of the epigraphs at the beginning of this book, I quote Jungian analyst Robert Johnson, who claims, "Everybody has a double duty in life, to maintain a cultural life and a religious life."[8] Johnson uses the term *cultural life* to refer to our actions and interactions, our behavior and our relationships. We have a duty to be good people—good to ourselves, to others, to animals, to the earth; good to all creatures and to all creation. By *religious life* Johnson does not mean faithfulness to a body of beliefs and practices, but a self-consciousness, a way of understanding ourselves that affirms that our humanity is infused with divinity.

It is my belief that the *cultural life* and the *religious life* are not unrelated but are the yin and yang of the moral life. For when we realize the full, sacred extent of our personhood, and when we live not from our ego but from our true, God-infused self (let go and let God), we will be in sync with the Tao, at one with God, in right relationship with the world, virtuous people, truly moral human beings.

Questions for Your Own Journey

Describe the feelings that accompanied your first exposure to moral teachings.

What positive purpose do moral teachings like the Ten Commandments and the Golden Rule have in your life?

Describe a time in your life when being true to the Spirit may have required you to go beyond the law.

How would you put into words the "moral" of your life? What life lessons have you learned? What meaning have you discovered by experiencing life's ups and downs?

8

What Problem of Evil?

> The Bible itself is filled with complaints of ill-treatment. From Moses, to Elijah, to the psalmist, to Job, to the Prophets, to Jesus himself, there goes up from its pages ... a persistent chorus of "How could you *do* this to me?" And yet God neither apologizes nor explains, and he certainly makes no effort to solve the problem of evil for them.
> —Robert Farrar Capon, *The Third Peacock*

The title of this chapter seems to imply that there may be no such thing as evil or that if there is, it is not a problem. I would not want to justify either conclusion to the victims of natural disasters, disease, inhumane treatment at the hands of another, or oppressive social structures. Whether large in scope, like the Holocaust, apartheid, and contemporary genocides, or less newsworthy but still painful occurrences, such as accidents, miscarriages, and abuse, life is full of both intentional and unintentional events and circumstances that bring untold suffering to thousands on a daily basis.

Most of us would prefer not to see life's dark side. It is scary to acknowledge that there is a malevolent power afoot that has the potential to wreak havoc in the world and especially in *our* world. Theologian Walter Wink writes about our reluctance to face the reality of evil, especially when it affects the most vulnerable among us:

> Most of us ... simply do not *want* to believe in radical evil. The implications are too terrible. It violates the reasonable, middle-class paradigm to learn that children are kidnapped for prostitution rings, Satan cults, and pornographic "snuff" movies (where actual murders are filmed).[1]

Our attempts to deny its existence notwithstanding, evil as a reality in the lives of individuals, organizations, and societies is without question both real and a problem, for if it does not result in loss of life, it often reduces life to a matter of enduring the struggle to survive in the face of pain.

The religious world in which I was raised taught that for reasons beyond my comprehension and that were none of my business, God allowed evil to exist. And when it came to my causing evil, well, "The devil made me do it." It was Satan in the form of a serpent who tempted Adam and Eve in the Garden (Genesis 3:1–5), and it was he, undisguised, who invited Jesus to worship him rather than God in the desert (Luke 4:1–13):

> Jesus, full of the Holy Spirit, returned from the Jordan and was led by the Spirit in the wilderness, where for forty days he was tempted by the devil. He ate nothing at all during those days, and when they were over, he was famished. The devil said to him, "If you are the Son of God, command this stone to become a loaf of bread." Jesus answered him, "It is written, 'One does not live by bread alone.'" Then the devil led him up and showed him in an instant all the kingdoms of the world. And the devil said to him, "To you I will give their glory and all this

authority; for it has been given over to me, and I give it to anyone I please. If you, then, will worship me, it will all be yours." Jesus answered him, "It is written, 'Worship the Lord your God, and serve only him.'" Then the devil took him to Jerusalem, and placed him on the pinnacle of the temple, saying to him, "If you are the Son of God, throw yourself down from here, for it is written, 'He will command his angels concerning you, to protect you,' and 'On their hands they will bear you up, so that you will not dash your foot against a stone.'" Jesus answered him, "It is said, 'Do not put the Lord your God to the test.'" When the devil had finished every test, he departed from him until an opportune time.

The Problem of God

The *problem of evil* is a phrase that most often refers not to the everyday reality of evil and its consequences but to its reality in relation to God. How can evil in its various forms exist if God is both loving and powerful? What kind of God would allow tragedy to occur? Where is God when bad things happen to good people? But it is precisely the God question that moves me to pose the query "What problem of evil?", for evil ceases to be a problem theologically when we recognize that our understanding of God is the problem!

I again refer to a response Bishop John Shelby Spong made on his website when he was asked the following question: "If God is all-loving, why do we have disasters like earthquakes, famine, and war?"

> I think the problem is actually located in the operative definition of God that people use unconsciously. I call that definition "Theism." Theism says that God is a Being ... who is supernatural in power, dwelling

somewhere outside this world ... and who periodi-
cally invades the world to accomplish the divine will.
It is that definition of God that, I believe, creates the
problem that elicits your question.[2]

I believe Spong is correct in saying that a theistic understanding
of God is the reason we are confounded by the reality of evil.
This is so, in part, because we project onto God our need to
have life make sense, have order, and be fair or just. When life is
otherwise—when, like a baseball pitcher, it serves up curveballs,
wild pitches, and beanballs—both we and our notion of God
may be thrown for a loop. But all the while it is just life being
what life is: apparently senseless, often chaotic, and downright
unfair.

A dramatic event that has forced many people to grapple
with the problem of evil was the earthquake that struck Haiti
in January 2010, a disaster that resulted in well over 300,000
deaths. In the days following this tragedy, representatives of
various faith traditions were asked by the media why God would
have caused, allowed, or not intervened to prevent this occur-
rence. The responses I heard ranged from those who believed
God was punishing the people who died to those who felt God
was either indifferent or powerless to prevent this disaster. I do
not recall hearing the response that I would have agreed with:
that the question presumed the existence of a God who doesn't
exist, a being apart from us, whose business it is to intervene in
the workings of the world.

I believe that earthquakes, tsunamis, and other devastating
natural phenomena are, in a sense, theologically neutral. The
earth is still in the throes of its evolutionary formation; we have
not seen the last of those explosive occurrences that both shape
and reshape the landscape of our planet. God is not absent from
this process but steeped in its burning layers. It is unfortunate,
to say the least, that we are often in the way of Earth's ongoing creation, but this has nothing to do with the intention or

indifference of a distant God. Rather, it has everything to do with creation's holy evolution and with its random and unfortunate consequences. But in the midst of all that we experience as disastrous, God's omnipresence accompanies us. I believe that God was buried in the rubble of Haiti that January day.

Turning toward or Away from God

The experience of life's trials and tragedies brings some people to believe in God as a Supreme Being, for it is in these situations that we can feel the need for a relationship with an entity we imagine to be more powerful than ourselves. That was the case for a woman I encountered in the hospital not long ago. Sheila was in her midforties and was in constant and intense pain as she faced serious back surgery. She told me about her concern for her son, a drug addict who could not hold a job; her daughter; who had a penchant for abusive relationships; and her alcoholic ex-husband, who had left her years ago but continued to disrupt her life with his angry outbursts and constant pleas for financial assistance. I was amazed at how upbeat Sheila was, despite her circumstances, and when I asked how she managed to maintain such a positive attitude, she replied that her situation had brought her to her knees. She said that she used to be angry at God for not sparing her the hardships she experienced, so she had turned away from God and religion years ago. But now, out of a sense of desperation, Sheila had begun praying to God and felt that doing so was helping her to cope. The saying "There are no atheists in foxholes" can apply to everyday life as well as to war.

There are many people who do not feel the comfort of God's presence in their darkness, as Sheila did. For some, God is a source of punishment. But rather than blaming God for the events that bring them suffering, they blame themselves. They think that if they had been better people, the tragedy they experienced would not have occurred. It is not uncommon to hear someone say, in the midst of difficult times, that they think God is punishing them for wrongs they had done or are now doing.

But people often turn away from God when their lives take a "wrong turn," for their understanding of God as loving, fair, and in charge is undermined by the evils they experience. I see this phenomenon as tragic and unnecessary, an evil in its own right. I see it as the fault of churches whose failure to educate their members beyond the images and stories that were appropriate in their childhoods has left these people without a theology that could serve them as adults. Such stories portray God as one who protects from harm those who are good and punishes all who are not. A better image, a story closer to the truth, would present God as an incarnate presence who, like a faithful and loving spouse, parent, or partner, accompanies us in life for better or for worse, in sickness and in health, through death and beyond.

The prevalence of evil can make it difficult to posit the existence of a caring, parentlike God, but this is the image that both the Hebrew and Christian Scriptures present:

> Does a woman forget the baby at the breast, or fail to
> cherish the son of her womb? Yet even if these forget,
> I will never forget you. (Isaiah 49:15)

> If you, then, who are evil, know how to give your chil-
> dren what is good, how much more will your Father
> in heaven give good things to those who ask him!
> (Matthew 7:11)

These biblical references indicate that in the Jewish and Christian traditions, God is thought to hover over humanity like a good, nurturing parent. Surely this is a difficult image for those who have experienced abuse and/or neglect at the hand of a mother or father. Such experiences are tragic precisely because parents are supposed to be loving and nurturing; they are supposed to promote health, security, and happiness, not undermine them.

But the parental metaphor used to describe God's relationship to humanity in the Bible is not to be taken literally. God does not take care of us the way a loving parent cares for children, attending to their every need. Instead, the notion that God is parental is to be understood spiritually; that is, God is one with us as a parent and child are one, no matter what. I have seen the pain in the eyes of parents as they stand by helpless at the bedside of their hospitalized child. They may feel responsible that their son or daughter is ill, for prevention and protection are deeply embedded instincts in every good parent. But the reality is that by their loving, compassionate, and helpless-to-help presence, parents give witness to the abiding truth that God is one with us through thick and thin.

Discovering God in the Midst of Evil

Theodicy is the defense of God's goodness and omnipotence in the face of evil. An apology of sorts, theodicy attempts to prove what has come into question, to make a case for God's benevolence despite evidence to the contrary. But when we realize that the problem of evil is a problem with our concept of God, theodicy becomes irrelevant. What is needed instead is a theology that allows God to exist *in the midst of evil*. Episcopal priest and theologian Robert Farrar Capon addresses this point:

> If God seems to be in no hurry to make the problem of evil go away, maybe we shouldn't be either. Maybe our compulsion to wash God's hands for him is a service he doesn't appreciate. Maybe—all theodicies and nearly all theologians to the contrary—*evil is where we meet God*.... Maybe—just maybe—if we ever solved the problem, we'd have talked ourselves out of a lover.[3]

In dealing with the problem of evil Capon is not interested in its origin or in the fact that evil calls God's presumed goodness and power into question. Rather, his concern—and mine—is that we not allow the reality of evil to blind us to the loving Presence present in and with us in our suffering. Evil has always been part of the human condition; why or whence it comes is of less interest to me than the wonder of discovering God in its midst.

I would venture to say that the vast majority of religions, Christian and otherwise, teach that God is capable of redirecting the course of events that we experience as tragic or hurtful. If we pray hard enough, make sufficient sacrifices, or get our lives straightened out, God just might work the magic that will turn things around. And so we are prone to bargain with God, promising, "If you get me through this, I'll go back to church, stop doing drugs, work at a soup kitchen," and so on.

I used to bargain with God in this fashion, and I found hope and consolation in the belief that intervention was possible. I do so no longer. Perhaps my current belief has been influenced by my disappointment in God's failure to respond as I would like, but what I really think is that my faith has matured beyond the instinctual desire to be spared from the sometimes harsh occurrences of life. Don't get me wrong, I still prefer pleasure over pain and joy over sorrow, but I have now come to embrace the reality of evil without the expectation of being delivered from it by divine intervention. I have also come to believe that the power of God lies not in the miraculous ability to right wrongs but in the sometimes undetectable yet enduring Presence that accompanies us in good times and in bad. Writing from the same notion of God that this book posits, Christian theologian Marcus Borg supports the idea of divine presence as opposed to divine intervention:

> Rather than speaking of divine intervention, panentheism speaks of divine intention and divine interaction. Or, to use sacramental language, it sees the presence of God "in, with, and under" everything—not as

the direct cause of events, but as a presence beneath
and within our everyday lives.[4]

In the Christian tradition, Jesus is believed to be the inflesh-
ment of God, the Divine Presence in human form. I have already
argued that affirming this only in relation to Jesus reflects a limited understanding of the notion of incarnation, but this teaching
does convey a truth about God that is basic to the Christian way.
God is within the human condition and is as powerless in the
face of evil as Jesus was. God is not in the business of intervention, prevention, or protection; rather, God's business is love.

It has been said that love is a harsh and dreadful thing. Love
is not only about romantic longings and passionate advances.
It also involves suffering with others, sharing their burdens,
and grieving their losses. This is love's way, and *Love*, we say, is
God's name. I refer again to Capon:

> Might not Incarnation be his response, not to the
> incidental irregularity of sin, but to the unhelpable
> presence of badness in creation?... When we are
> helpless, there he is. He doesn't start your stalled car
> for you: he comes and dies with you in the snowbank.
> You can object that he should have made a world
> in which cars don't stall; but you can't complain he
> doesn't stick by his customers.[5]

In this anthropomorphic analogy, Capon is claiming what I have
argued in a more mystical vein: that God is inseparable from
creation. Feelings of abandonment in time of need are normal
enough, since most of us have internalized a theistic concept of
God as all-powerful and because we are often powerless in the
face of evil. But the reality is that because God is the spiritual
Ground of our being, we are never alone. We are never without
the presence of the Divine in the midst of the inevitability of
evil. I don't recommend trying to convince people of this truth

if they are in physical, emotional, or spiritual pain; rather, I suggest that you embody its truth by being a comforting presence in their plight—actions have always spoken louder than words, and they always will.

We Are Agents of Evil

Having made a case for the possibility that God's coexistence with the reality of evil is a problem only because of our understanding of who God is (a Supreme Being) and how God operates (intervention), I must also address the fact of our agency in relation to evil. Apart from natural disasters ("acts of God," in the lexicon of the insurance industry), evil can exist only through us. Spiritual writer and psychiatrist Gerald May, using the term *violence* for the most part, states a litany of the ways in which we cause pain and suffering to one another:

> There's completely accidental violence, violence that comes from carelessness, reasoned and premeditated violence, impulsive violence, violence for sport, mindless violence under its own unknown power, and pure cruelty, evil for evil's sake.[6]

There is no devil that makes us do anything. Rather, it is our actions or our failure to act—whether conscious or unconscious, intended or unintended, the result of our perversity or our mental or emotional incapacity—that is the cause of many of the evils that spawn suffering. Centuries of moral teachings that stressed the inevitability of God's punishment if we did not "do good and avoid evil" have failed to stem the tide of humanity's inhumanity. Despite our best efforts and our worst fears, we continue to perpetrate evil intrapersonally (we afflict ourselves by means of self-criticism), interpersonally (we inflict pain on others by word and deed), and internationally (we engage in conflicts of war and other forms of political, economic, and social aggression).

Whether it has to do with the existence of evil or the existence of evildoers, the problem is the same: our misconceptions of God. In the first instance, the existence of evil, the problem is the false notion that God is all-powerful and thus able to redirect life in order to bring about happy, successful outcomes in the face of overwhelming odds. In the second instance, the fact that we are the perpetrators of evil, the problem is our failure to be aware of and to act in accordance with the truth that God dwells within. This is a perspective held by psychologist and Merton scholar James Finley, who writes:

> For I doubt very much that we would do all the things
> we do to abandon and hurt ourselves and others if
> we lived in perpetual awareness of our preciousness
> as persons subsisting in the love that is our very life.[7]

It may be simplistic, but I believe that our tendency to inflict evil on ourselves or others is most often the result of our failure to know with our minds and hearts the truth of God's indwelling. This is our sin, both individually and collectively, and the source of many of the evils that plague us. When we are not attuned to the divinity of our humanity, our attitudes and actions often fail to give witness to our God-Self. Author and psychoanalyst Thomas Moore refers to this disconnect as "loss of soul":

> The great malady of the twentieth century implicated
> in all our troubles and affecting us individually and
> socially is "loss of soul." When soul is neglected it
> doesn't go away, it appears symptomatically in obses-
> sions, addictions, violence, and loss of meaning.[8]

I find it impossible to read the morning paper or watch the evening news without coming to the conclusion that loss of soul is a reality. But if we have lost our souls—or lost touch with them— how can we find them again? How is it possible to reconnect with the divinity that is the bottom line of our being? I believe we can do so only if we are willing to be quietly with ourselves in a nonjudgmental and compassionate way.

Learning to Abide Ourselves

It has been said that the source of all violence is a person's inability to sit still in a room. Until I am able to abide my brokenness, I will continue to be an agent of evil, despite my best efforts. I have experienced this over and over again in my own life. I am at odds with others when I am not at peace with myself. I am impatient with others when I demand of myself that I be the ideal person I may never become. I know I am not alone in this; I have been privy to its truth in others many times in counseling situations. Although the cause is not always to be found there, the first place to look when we are in conflict with another is within ourselves. But the willingness to stop and look inside requires courage, humility, and the discipline to resist the urge to busy ourselves and distract ourselves so as not to feel our discontent.

The scriptural basis for being discontent with ourselves and for the havoc this can wreak is found in the myth of Adam and Eve's fall from grace. The story has it that they were tempted by the serpent to eat the fruit of the tree that would give them all knowledge; if they ate from this tree, they would become like God. They were tempted by the implication that being who they were was not sufficient. They were made to feel discontented with their humanity.

Like all myths, the story of Adam and Eve's fall tells an eternal truth evident in the hearts of all people. There lurks within each of us a deep dissatisfaction with ourselves, the gnawing sense that we would be happier and that life would be better if we were different. This is sometimes referred to as the "if-only syndrome." If only I were taller or shorter. If only I were thinner or heavier. If only I were smarter, more talented, less shy, more holy, and so on. When we fall prey to the temptation to strive for perfection or to achieve an ideal without first realizing God's indwelling, we end up "outside the garden" and create dissonance within ourselves and disharmony in the world around us.

Objectively speaking, evil is a problem whose consequences we are called to address. Theologically speaking, evil is a problem that invites us to reassess our notion of God as a being apart from humanity. Personally speaking, we become the perpetrators of evil when we fail to embrace ourselves as people who embody God in our less-than-perfect selves.

Questions for Your Own Journey

How do you try to make sense of the fact that evil is so ever-present?

What, if any, incongruence is there between your notion of God and the existence of evil?

How has your experience of life's difficulties affected your beliefs about God?

Have you ever experienced the loving presence of God in the midst of suffering? If so, describe what that was like.

9

Church with a Mission, Mission with a Church

> How is the Church, as an earthly association, related
> to the eschatological entity of the kingdom of heav-
> en?... We must take care not to get caught in the false
> disjunction between structure and function. These
> cannot be separated, and neither of them can be
> absolutized at the expense of the other.... Each must
> receive some weight if the Church is to have both
> solidarity and the dynamism necessary to her health.
> —John Macquarrie, *Principles of Christian Theology*

I conclude our consideration of religious teachings with this chapter on the church because it is so instrumental in form-ing the beliefs that shape our lives and because, like all human organizations, the church stands in need of reform from time to time. Nowhere have I seen this put more clearly than in the words of the contemporary Jewish spiritual leader Rabbi Zalman Schachter-Shalomi:

> Every tradition begins in the white heat of tran-
> scendent realization, then gradually over time

suffers hardening of the religious arteries through
the unavoidable process of institutionalization.[1]

Recast in the form of a question, the title of this chapter asks, "Is the church primarily an institution that puts organizational image and requirements before the needs of those it serves, or does the corporate structure exist to enable and enhance the ministry offered through it?" My answer to both parts of this question is yes, for both structure and ministry are important aspects of all religious institutions.

Before I go any further, let me say that because I write from the perspective of a lifelong Catholic, it is my experience of the Catholic Church that colors what I think and say about this topic. However, I am aware that my experience is not unlike that of people raised in other faith traditions, Christian and otherwise. As unique as each tradition is, all religious institutions are faced with the necessity of attending not only to the needs of individuals but also to the infrastructure that allows them to maintain houses of worship, provide social and other services to their membership, and promote their brand to ensure a vital future through sustained and increased membership.

Church or Mission: Which Comes First?

A church with a mission ("church/mission") is an organization not unlike a corporation; it is a political entity that is often powerful and wealthy, has a structure and an infrastructure, and has investors, investments, and a payroll. Church/mission requires time, attention, and both human and financial resources in order to function. And, like other organizations, it sometimes loses sight of its mission, which, in the case of Christian churches, is to be the visible sign of Christ by tending to the physical, emotional, and spiritual needs of humankind.

A mission with a church ("mission/church"), in contrast is a living entity whose structure supports its dynamism in the same way that riverbanks channel the flow of water. Mission/church is a movement consisting of a community of believers who share a common faith and set of values and whose attitude toward rules, regulations, and rubrics is flexible, not rigid. There is room for exceptions; the guiding principle is that people come before principles.

I find it tempting to bash a church/mission because it can be so impersonal. The concern of this church for its own structure, operation, and reputation may appear to be the cart before the horse or the tail that wags the dog. Should not the mission come first? Are not the needs of people more important than institutional priorities? Didn't Jesus indicate that the Spirit is more important than the letter of the law, and that, as stated in Mark 2:27, "The Sabbath is made for man, not man for the Sabbath"?

Because I know that the question we are pondering is not an either-or and because, as the epigraph at the beginning of this chapter suggests, the structure and mission of the church can complement each other, I will resist the temptation to focus exclusively on the flaws of the church understood as institution. I will not dwell for long on the bureaucratic brick wall that has inflicted bumps and bruises on many who have sought solace at its door, but I must pay some attention to this reality because to do otherwise might give the impression that its faults are inconsequential.

When Church Comes First

When church comes before mission, when institutional identity precedes ministry to the masses, I believe the church loses sight of its purpose. I question whether my religion, Catholicism, has lost its raison d'être when, in keeping with the letter of the law, women are denied the possibility of ordination, non-Catholic Christians are not allowed to receive the Eucharist, full-fledged Catholics are told they may not receive communion if they vote for political candidates who do not support the Catholic view on social issues, homosexuals are labeled "disordered," and, in order to preserve an untarnished image, abusive clergy are reassigned rather than rehabilitated (if indeed that is even possible). Truly, in these and other matters, the institutional church not only supersedes its mission but obliterates it. I believe this is a major cause of the exodus of so many from the Catholic Church. The U.S. Religious Landscape Survey, conducted by the Pew Forum in November 2012, states that one-third of survey respondents who say they were raised Catholic no longer describe themselves as Catholic—nearly 10 percent of all Americans are former Catholics.

Church/mission was the church of my youth. I was born and lived into my late teenage years under the influence of the pre–Vatican II church. This was the church of Rome, of the pope, and of the hierarchy and other clergy, an institution whose teachings were not to be questioned but were to be believed with blind faith. Its God was the God of theism, the Supreme Being who both created and judged all that "He" had made.

This was the church of the *Baltimore Catechism*, a book that posed questions and provided answers regarding every aspect of religion; it was a book that most Catholics in my generation felt obligated to memorize. This church imposed a heavy-handed morality on its members that spelled out the many ways in which one could sin against God and therefore deserve eternal punishment.

The Catholic Church of this era presented itself as the one true church outside which there was no salvation (*extra ecclesiam nulla salus*); its sacraments were *the* means of attaining God's grace. There was little doubt in the minds of Catholics influenced by this understanding of church that they were God's favorites, that Protestants ran a distant second, and that all non-Christians were off God's radar screen altogether.

The church's focus on power, control, and self-preservation as described above often overshadows its mission and its history as a powerful force for good. Through organized efforts, the Catholic Church attends to the needs of the poor, sick, unemployed, undocumented, homeless, helpless, hapless masses. Both hands-on help and the challenging of systemic evils that oppress the most vulnerable among us are addressed through its pronouncements and programs. Yet despite the church's having been a beacon in the darkness for centuries, the lingering sense of countless Catholics in my generation is that a church/mission is at least as concerned about maintaining power and image as it is about assisting those in need.

Of course, it is not only the Catholic Church that struggles with image, power, and control, on the one hand, and ministry, on the other. The Episcopal Church and the Evangelical Lutheran Church in America, for instance, both experience a great deal of conflict over same-sex marriage and the ordination of gays and women as bishops; in some cases, these issues have even led to schism.

Mission First: Back to the Future

As I write, the church/mission approach is still very prevelent in our culture; however, since the days of my late adolescence, a mission/church perspective has been on the rise. Having entered the seminary during the Second Vatican Council—an event that signaled the beginning of a new and more progressive era in Catholicism—I was close to the action when it came to hearing about and studying the documents that emerged from that conclave. It was a case of "back to the future," in the sense that the spirit of Vatican II was a return to the spirit that characterized the movement that arose in the wake of Jesus's life: a spirit of vitality, compassion, and inclusivity.

Most scripture scholars agree that it was never Jesus's intention to establish a new religion. The mission he assumed as he became aware of the incarnate nature of God was the reform of his own religious tradition; he was sent to the "lost sheep of the house of Israel" (Matthew 15:24). The early followers of Jesus were known as "the Way." They made up a movement that came into being in response to Jesus's charismatic presence and persuasive preaching. There were various groupings of his followers: local sympathizers who came to hear Jesus whenever he was in their region, disciples who followed him from place to place, and the inner circle of apostles who were called to a deeper intimacy by him. It would be fair to characterize Jesus's followers as a loose affiliation of misfits: Jews who were no longer fed spiritually by Judaism; gentiles who felt affirmed by Jesus, despite their second-class status in Jewish eyes; certain kind of sinners; and the poor—all of whom were given a sense of hope by Jesus's message and his manner toward them.

The gist of Jesus's message had to do with the personal and compassionate nature of God, whom he referred to as his *abba* ("father"); the dignity of all people, no matter what their religious beliefs or life circumstances; and the primacy of love over the law. Many point to the Beatitudes (Matthew 5:3–12) as the manifesto of the movement his life generated:

> Blessed are the poor in spirit, for theirs is the kingdom of heaven.
> Blessed are those who mourn, for they will be comforted.
> Blessed are the meek, for they will inherit the earth.
> Blessed are those who hunger and thirst for righteousness, for they will be filled.
> Blessed are the merciful, for they will receive mercy.
> Blessed are the pure in heart, for they will see God.
> Blessed are the peacemakers, for they will be called children of God.
> Blessed are those who are persecuted for righteousness's sake, for theirs is the kingdom of heaven.
> Blessed are you when people revile you and persecute you and utter all kinds of evil against you falsely on my account.
> Rejoice and be glad, for your reward is great in heaven, for in the same way they persecuted the prophets who were before you.

Mission/church is far from being a flawless entity, but it is a community of believers who are filled with the Spirit that infused Jesus and his followers. Mission/church is more spiritual than religious in the institutional sense. Its adherents see themselves as related spiritually to all humanity, not just to those who share their beliefs about Jesus or who engage in the devotional practices of their faith tradition.

Because people come before principles in the mission/church model, compassion is more important than compliance with rules and regulations. I once overheard a statement made by a progressive bishop that speaks to this point. In response to the accusation that he was soft on abortion, he said, "I'm not soft on abortion, I'm soft on people." This is reminiscent of Jesus's words to the woman who was to be stoned:

> "Where are they? Is there no one left to condemn you?... Well, then," Jesus said, "I do not condemn you either." (John 8:10–11)

In Defense of Cafeteria Christians

Although many mission/church adherents continue to value and to participate in church services and activities, those who put mission before church tend not to embrace every teaching or practice of their faith family. In my tradition, they are pejoratively called "cafeteria Catholics." Poet and Catholic convert Mary Karr identifies herself with this group:

> While probably not the late Pope's favorite Catholic (nor he my favorite Pope), I took the blessing and ate the broken bread. And just as I continue to live in America and vote despite my revulsion for many U.S. policies, I continue to take the sacraments despite my fervent aversion to certain doctrines. Call me a cafeteria Catholic if you like, but to that I'd say, who isn't?[2]

Those who criticize this approach see such people as both self-ish and irresponsible, taking only what they want, believing only what makes sense to them, doing what comes easy. But, in my experience, many of these people are thoughtful and live with a great deal of faith and integrity. Yes, they are selective when it comes to teachings and devotional practices, but they act out of a sense of responsibility, accountability to the Spirit, and the desire to live authentic spiritual lives. They are not so much cutting corners as they are walking a path that feeds their souls.

This way of being religious might be considered a slippery slope, open to comfort but closed to challenge. It is true that some cafeteria types do not consider the good of the community when they decide to be absent from communal gatherings; they have forgotten that their absence as well as their presence affects the whole. But a blanket condemnation of those who are selective in their beliefs and practices dismisses the possibility that the Spirit can work with and in us no matter how much we may have wandered from orthodoxy. In fact, it may even *be* the Spirit that leads us beyond religious convention, as it did Jesus.

Not unlike Jesus in his relationship to Judaism, some people find that when they begin to value and attend to their spiritual development, they feel at odds with institutional religion. This unfortunate reality was referred to by several people who wrote to me after reading my book *A Faith Worth Believing*. One man said, "I've never felt so close to God and so far from the church." And a woman wrote the following:

> I am a lifelong Catholic and I am currently active in my parish, yet I often feel lost and alone.... I feel hypocritical for no longer being able to embrace Catholicism without question.... It seems that the more spiritual I try to become, the less Catholic I become.

These are not statements by disloyal, faithless people; rather, they are testimonies from people whose love for God, the church, and their souls has moved them to recognize that no religion has a monopoly on the truth and that they must follow the Spirit's lead, no matter where it takes them.

Culture versus Consciousness

I have found that the church that puts its organizational needs before its mission does a worse job at what Jungian analyst Robert Johnson considers the church's first responsibility:

> The duty of the church (whatever the creed) should be to assist people with their religious life, which involves seeing past duality and advancing conscious-ness. The cultural life consists of choosing between good and evil and keeping the human side of life in order and proportion. So many religious institutions today focus on the cultural life almost exclusively instead of helping people cultivate a different kind of consciousness.[3]

My experience supports Johnson's claim that most religious institutions emphasize the cultural life. It's all about our moral and social responsibility, how we ought to relate to the individuals we encounter and the groups to which we belong. This is not only an important aspect of religion but also one that is necessary, for faith that is not anchored in the realities of our day-to-day lives and relationships is idealistic at best and useless at worse. But the edifice of "cultural life" rests on the foundation of "religious life," that higher consciousness or self-understanding that affirms humanity's divinity. The primary task of any religious organization is to tell us who we are (spiritual beings), not just how we should act.

Because a church/mission focuses on the concrete reality of organizational life, there is a tendency to speak concretely not only about morals but also about money. I have spoken to many disappointed and frustrated churchgoers who complain that what they hear about most often from the pulpit is not an affirmation of their worth but the importance of sharing their wealth. These people do not begrudge the fact that it takes money for a church to function; the source of their dissatisfaction lies in what they experience as the church's lack of response to their spiritual needs. There should never be a question in people's minds that churches are more concerned with their being aligned with God than they are about the "bottom line."

Church and Mission: Partners, Not Adversaries

I have already mentioned that the church's mission has to do primarily with meeting humanity's physical, emotional, and spiritual needs. As individuals, each of us can do something to bring to those in need what they require in order to make life more tolerable. But when we pool our resources with the help of the structure of the church, more can happen for a greater number of people. The gospel account of the multiplication of loaves in Matthew 14:15–21 is an illustration of this truth. This story tells of Jesus feeding thousands of people with only a few loaves of bread and some fish. It is commonly viewed as a miraculous event that demonstrates Jesus's power and compassion, but another interpretation is that the miracle was not Jesus's ability to feed the hungry throng with next to nothing, but his ability to elicit the generosity of those who had enough to feed themselves and were inclined to do only that. It was their willingness to share the little they had that enabled everyone to have his or her fill.

If people are hungry and homeless, the church's mission is to feed and shelter them. But where our individual efforts may assist a few, the existence of food banks, soup kitchens, and houses of hospitality facilitate this mission on a grand scale. When people are lost and lonely, we can stand by them, but it's good to know that there are professionals available at pastoral counseling centers. Healing is the mission when people are sick. In many communities, churches sponsor hospitals whose mission is to care for the whole person: body, mind, and spirit. Likewise, churches have been instrumental in the ministry of education by establishing schools at every level.

It is probably obvious that I believe the mission of the church is more important than its structure; however, the mission is less effective without the presence and power of the institution. I witnessed a simple example of this one Sunday morning while entering the hospital where I worked. A young woman and a child were crossing the street hand in hand on their way to the church located across from the hospital. The little girl was carrying a plastic shopping bag containing what appeared to be several cans of food. Many churches encourage the contribution of foodstuffs, which, when collected, are then distributed to the hungry or to organizations that feed them. It occurred to me that the organizational structure of this particular church was instrumental in eliciting and guiding the generous impulses of this woman and her child. Despite their shortcomings, churches continue to help their constituents live gospel values.

The structure and the mission of the church are sometimes in conflict—a house divided. But the church is at its best when living with the tension of organizational requirements and the mission to serve. When both are honored, those in greatest need will be more likely to receive what they require, and the "Kindom" (web of loving relationships) of God will be closer to becoming a reality.

Questions for Your Own Journey

What reforms do you think are needed in your religious tradition and/or in churches in general?

If you once belonged to a church, why did you leave? What would be required in order for you to return to communal religious practice?

What is your experience of church regarding cultural versus religious or spiritual life?

Which have you heard more about from the pulpit, "good and evil" or the idea that we are spiritual beings?

∽

Epilogue
A Spiritual Epoch
on the Rise

We shall not cease from exploration
And the end of all our exploring
Will be to arrive where we started
And know the place for the first time.
                        —T. S. Eliot, "Four Quartets"

As we conclude our exploration though the pages of this book, I would like to return momentarily to where we started. While this work was still in the manuscript stage, I asked my friend Jim Finley to read the introduction. His feedback helped me understand what I was attempting to do as I invited my readers to look anew at religious truths and where my passion for doing so is situated in the context of our times.

Referring to the work of philosopher Reiner Schurmann, Jim spoke of the threefold energy of epochs. Every epoch has an arising energy, a sustaining energy, and a declining energy. As I see it, we in the Western world are living in a transitional time between an epoch of religion that is on the decline and an epoch of spirituality that is on the rise. This is a dynamic that has occurred repeatedly throughout history. The traditional interpretation of religious truths and the institutional church that has been a mouthpiece for them are losing both credibility and influence with countless numbers of people, many of whom claim that they are not religious, but are spiritual, and are now searching for God beyond religion and outside church.

Epochs die hard. There is a sense in which many religious institutions refuse to acknowledge the presence and power of the arising spiritual epoch. Instead of being in dialogue with it, they take an adversarial stance and are quick to label its beliefs and believers "heretical" or "New Age." They view this epoch as Godless, its philosophy devoid of values, and its adherents in need of returning to the fold.

Churches that have this attitude are missing the opportunity to feed the spiritually hungry at their doors. I am not suggesting that there is no value in the tradition or that churches should compromise themselves in order to achieve relevance in the minds of those who have turned from their teachings. On the contrary, the church's voices proclaiming the primacy of life in what has been called our "culture of death" and its insistence on simplicity and generosity in our culture of materialism are instances of its being what it should be: prophetic. However, it is both possible and, I believe, preferable to be radically prophetic without being deliberately antagonistic. After all, churches are part of the culture whose values they ought to challenge.

In stark contrast to this, the ethos of the arising spiritual epoch is based on the belief that this life, our world, and the flawed culture in which we find ourselves is the venue of God. It may not always appear so, but beneath the marred surface of creation and the uncomely aspects of our humanity lurks an essential holiness.

What I think is needed is that religious institutions begin to listen and respond with open minds and hearts to the spiritual needs of their constituents. A spiritual epoch is on the rise. It is embodied in those who have a hunger to find meaning in the ordinary circumstances of life, who have a growing awareness that God is bigger than the doctrines and devotions of any faith tradition, and who feel a sense of oneness with all people that cuts through religious differences. The religious epoch would be revitalized if it welcomed and affirmed those who believe in and are passionate about such things.

Phil Jackson, a professional basketball coach and devotee of a Zen-like approach to life, has said that he looks upon opposing teams not as enemies but as dancing partners! The emerging spiritual epoch has learned to dance with the world, for it recognizes and honors the partnership that unites sacred and secular, heaven and earth, humanity and divinity. If traditional religion does not learn this dance, it will surely die; it has already done so in the minds and hearts of many who embrace the arising epoch and who are committed to the life it promises.

Those of us who hunger for spiritual meaning in the routine of our lives seek God in the world. We may not be fully conscious of or articulate about what we believe, but like an animal with its nose to the ground, we are following the scent of the sacred along roads less traveled, knowing that we are on the trail of something worth pursuing. I hope that if you didn't have it before reading this book, you may have picked up the scent of the divine as you made your way through its pages. The sacred is in our midst.

What I am coming to realize is that being spiritually alive is not a matter of discovering and devouring our prey (God), but of being on the hunt. Every day, and every event and encounter that unfolds within it, is replete with the divinity for which we long. When we honor and embrace our longing rather than grasping for a set of beliefs to satisfy it, we find ourselves strangely content in our discontent, fed by our own hunger, enlivened by our exploration, and surprised anew when we return to the place from which we started: the primal place that is God's indwelling presence in the midst of ourselves and of all creation.

Ours is an exciting, albeit trying, time. We straddle two epochs. We are a dimension of the dance of God. My prayer is that we will hear the music, feel its force, and move with it into the future, where we will join with the dancers of all creeds and cultures to form one vast body that respects religious differences and moves beyond the antipathy and division those differences have caused.

~

Acknowledgments

I relish this opportunity to give a "shout out," a word of recognition and gratitude for the many people who have assisted me in bringing this book to completion. There are, indeed, many fingerprints on its pages that are not mine.

I thank the too-many-to-count seekers who have shared their journeys with me in spiritual direction. It has been a privilege to hear their stories and to witness the sincerity of their quest for God.

My gratitude goes out to the "Mystics of Maine" (Sherry Flint, Suzy Hallett, Carol Thompson, Windy Wickenden), who have welcomed me many times not only to their beautiful state, but into their lives as well. My connection with them has put flesh on the term "spiritual friend."

The following people have invested time and energy into reading the manuscript and giving me honest feedback about it: Ray DeFabio, Dave Kopp, Mauro and Carrol Pando, Fritz and Carolyn Pfotenhauer, Bob Raccuglia, Suzanne Schellenbarger, John, Aurelia, and Scott Stella. I so appreciate their input and encouragement.

Jim Finley, whom I quote often, has been a major influence in the way I think about the spiritual life. His books, CDs, and friendship have, for over thirty years, been a source of sustenance for my soul. He has been the mentor to me that Thomas Merton was to him.

Special thanks to Amy McCord for everything from emotional support to technical assistance. She held my hand when I was discouraged and put her own hands to the keyboard when mine were inept. She is the companion of my heart and has helped me recognize the nearness of God.

I am grateful to Stuart M. Matlins, the publisher at SkyLight Paths, and to the many competent people there whose calling is to make good manuscripts into better books. Emily Wichland, my editor, did just that with gentle patience as I at times resisted her insightful suggestions. Additionally, assistant editor Kaitlin Johnstone, cover designer Heather Pelham, interior designer Kelley Barton, and publicist Kelly O'Neill—thank you for being so skilled at what you do.

Notes

Introduction

1. Jelaluddin Rumi, *The Essential Rumi*, trans. Coleman Barks with John Moyer (New York: HarperCollins, 1996), p. 36.

2. Annie Dillard, *For the Time Being* (New York: Vintage Books, 1999), pp. 169–70.

3. Gerard Manley Hopkins, *Poems of Gerard Manley Hopkins*, ed. W. H. Gardner, 3rd ed. (New York: Oxford University Press, 1948), p. 70.

1. God Beyond Religion

1. Joseph Campbell, *Thou Art That*, ed. Eugene Kennedy (Novato, CA: New World Library, 2001), p. 17.

2. John O'Donohue, *Anam Cara* (New York: Cliff Street Books, 1997), p. xvii.

3. Michael Himes, *Doing the Truth in Love* (Mahwah, NJ: Paulist Press, 1995), p. 9.

4. Mother Teresa, *Mother Teresa: Come Be My Light* (New York: Doubleday, 2007), p. 210.

5. Roger Housden, ed., *Ten Poems to Set You Free*, (New York: Harmony Books, 2003), p. 125.

2. What Becomes of Prayer If There Is No God?

1. The *Baltimore Catechism*, formerly known as *A Catechism of Christian Doctrine, Prepared and Enjoined by Order of the Third Council*

of Baltimore, was the first catechism written for Catholics in North America and became the standard Catholic school text in the United States from 1885 to the late 1960s. Though still used today in some Catholic schools, it fell out of popularity with the move away from catechism-based education.

2. John Shelby Spong, *A New Christianity for a New World* (San Francisco: HarperSanFrancisco, 2001), pp. 196–97.

3. Thomas Merton, *Day of a Stranger* (Salt Lake City, UT: Gibbs M. Smith, 1981), p. 41.

4. James Finley, *Christian Meditation* (San Francisco: HarperSanFrancisco, 2004), p. 7.

5. Jack Kornfield, *After the Ecstasy, the Laundry* (New York: Bantam Books, 2000), p. 290.

3. From Belief to Faith

1. Marcus Borg, *The Heart of Christianity* (San Francisco: HarperSanFrancisco, 2003), pp. 30–31.

2. Roger Housden, *Ten Poems to Change Your Life* (New York: Harmony Books, 2001), p. 18.

3. Quoted in James Fowler, *Stages of Faith* (San Francisco: Harper & Row, 1981), p. 31.

4. Elaine Pagels, *Beyond Belief* (New York: Random House, 2003), pp. 184–85.

4. Jesus: The Way, or in the Way?

1. Borg, *The Heart of Christianity*, pp. 87–88.

2. Ibid., pp. 86–87.

3. Martin Buber, *Tales of the Hasidim* (New York: Schocken Books, 1975), p. 251.

4. Quoted in Joel Porte, ed., *Emerson in His Journals* (Cambridge, MA: Harvard University Press, 1982), p. 126.

5. Why Didn't Someone Tell Me I'm a Mystic?

1. Kerry Walters, *Rufus Jones: Essential Writings* (Maryknoll, NY: Orbis Books, 2001), p. 18.

2. Finley, *Christian Meditation*, pp. 186–87.

3. Thomas Merton, *New Seeds of Contemplation* (New York: New Dimensions, 1972), p. 36.

4 Pagels, *Beyond Belief*, p. 34.

5. C. S. Lewis, *Surprised by Joy* (New York: Harcourt Brace, 1956), p. 226.

6. Annie Dillard, *Teaching a Stone to Talk* (New York: HarperCollins, 1982), pp. 94–95.

7. Roger Housden, ed., *Ten Poems to Open Your Heart* (New York: Harmony Books, 2003), pp. 117–18.

6. Inspiration Is Not Dictation

1. Annie Dillard, *Pilgrim at Tinker Creek* (New York: HarperCollins, 1974), p. 13.

2. Borg, *The Heart of Christianity*, pp. 13, 45.

3. www.johnshelbyspong.com

4. Sam Keen, *Hymns to an Unknown God* (New York: Bantam Books, 1994), p. 54.

5. Borg, *The Heart of Christianity*, p. 50.

6. Housden, ed., *Ten Poems to Set You Free*, pp. 55–56.

7. Joseph Campbell, *Thou Art That*, ed. Eugene Kennedy (Novato, CA: New World Library, 2001), pp. xvi–xvii.

7. Morality As Right Relationship

1. Gerald May, *The Wisdom of Wilderness* (San Francisco: HarperSanFrancisco, 2006), pp. xx–xxi.

2. The *Baltimore Catechism*, formerly known as *A Catechism of Christian Doctrine, Prepared and Enjoined by Order of the Third Council of Baltimore*, was the first catechism written for Catholics in North America and became the standard Catholic school text in the United States from 1885 to the late 1960s. Though still used today in some Catholic schools, it fell out of popularity with the move away from catechism-based education.

3. Quoted in Jon Winokur, *The Portable Curmudgeon* (New York: New American Library, 1987), p. 198.

4. William Johnston, *The Cloud of Unknowing* (New York: Doubleday, 1973), p. 23.

5. Thomas Merton, *The Way of Chuang Tzu* (Boston: Shambhala Publications, 1992), p. 26.

6. Thomas Merton, *The Sign of Jonas* (New York: Image Books, 1956), p. 54.

7. Parker Palmer, *Let Your Life Speak* (San Francisco: Jossey-Bass, 2000), pp. 66–69.

8. Robert Johnson, *Balancing Heaven and Earth* (San Francisco: HarperSanFrancisco, 1998), p. 173.

8. What Problem of Evil?

1. Walter Wink, *Engaging the Powers* (Minneapolis, MN: Fortress Press, 1992), p. 69.

2. www.johnshelbyspong.com

3. Robert Farrar Capon, *The Third Peacock* (Minneapolis, MN: Winston Press, 1986).

4. Borg, *The Heart of Christianity*, pp. 66–67.

5. Capon, *The Third Peacock*, pp. 63–64.

6. May, *The Wisdom of Wilderness*, p. 113.

7. Finley, *Christian Meditation*, p. 197.

8. Thomas Moore, *Care of the Soul* (New York: HarperCollins, 1992), p. xi.

9. Church with a Mission, Mission with a Church

1. Quoted in Ronald S. Miller, *As Above So Below* (Los Angeles: Jeremy P. Tarcher), p. 58.

2. Mary Karr, *Sinners Welcome* (New York: HarperCollins, 2006), p. 69.

3. Johnson, *Balancing Heaven and Earth*, p. 173.

Suggestions for Further Reading

Baum, Gregory. *Man Becoming*. New York: Herder & Herder, 1971.

Borg, Marcus. *The Heart of Christianity*. San Francisco: HarperCollins, 2003.

Buber, Martin. *Tales of the Hasidim*. New York: Schocken Books, 1975.

Campbell, Joseph. *Thou Art That*. Edited by Eugene Kennedy. Novato, CA: New World Library, 2001.

Capon, Robert Farrar. *The Third Peacock*. Minneapolis: Winston Press, 1986.

A Catechism of Christian Doctrine. revised edition of *The Baltimore Catechism*, no. 2. Paterson, NJ: St. Anthony Guild Press, 1954.

Dillard, Annie. *Pilgrim at Tinker Creek*. New York: HarperCollins, 1974.

———.*Teaching A Stone to Talk*. New York: HarperCollins, 1982.

Eliot, T. S. *Collected Poems 1909–1962*. New York: Harcourt, Brace & World, Inc., 1970.

Finley, James. *Christian Meditation*. San Francisco: HarperCollins, 2004.

Fowler, James. *Stages of Faith*. San Francisco: HarperCollins, 1981.

Himes, Michael. *Doing the Truth in Love*. Mahwah, NJ: Paulist Press, 1995.

Hopkins, Gerard Manley. *Poems of Gerard Manley Hopkins*. Edited by W. H. Gardner (3rd edition). New York: Oxford Press, 1948.

Housden, Roger. *Ten Poems to Change Your Life*. New York: Harmony Books, 2001.

———. *Ten Poems to Open Your Heart*. New York: Harmony Books, 2002.

———. *Ten Poems to Set You Free*. New York: Harmony Books, 2003.

Johnson, Robert. *Balancing Heaven and Earth*. San Francisco: HarperCollins, 1998.

Johnston, William. ed., *The Cloud of Unknowing*. New York: Doubleday, 1973.

Jones, Rufus, and Kerry Walters, *Rufus Jones: Essential Writings*. Maryknoll, NY: Orbis Books, 2001.

Karr, Mary. *Sinners Welcome*. New York: HarperCollins Publishers, 2006.

Keen, Sam. *Hymns to an Unknown God*. New York: Bantam Books, 1994.

Kornfield, Jack. *After the Ecstasy, the Laundry*. New York: Bantam Books, 2000.

Lewis, C.S. *Surprised By Joy*. New York: Harcourt Brace, 1956.

Macquairrie, John. *Principles of Christian Theology*. New York: Scribner, 1966.

May, Gerald. *The Wisdom of Wilderness*. San Francisco: Harper Collins, 2006.

Merton, Thomas. *Day of a Stranger*. Salt Lake City: Gibbs M. Smith, Inc., 1981.

———. *New Seeds of Contemplation*. New York: New Directions, 1972.

———. *The Sign of Jonas*. New York: Image Books, 1956.

———. *The Way of Chuang Tzu*. Boston: Shambhala Press, 1992.

Miller, Ronald S. *As Above So Below*. Los Angeles: Jeremy P. Tarcher, Inc., 1992.

Moore, Thomas. *Care of the Soul*. New York: HarperCollins, 1992.

O'Donohue, John. *Anam Cara: A Book of Celtic Wisdom*. New York: HarperCollins, 1998.

Pagels, Elaine. *Beyond Belief*. New York: Random House, 2003.

Palmer, Parker. *Let Your Life Speak*. San Francisco: Jossey-Bass, 2000.

Porte, Joel. ed., *Emerson in His Journals*. Cambridge, MA: Harvard University Press, 1982.

Rumi, Jelaluddin. *The Essential Rumi*. Translated by Coleman Barks with John Moyer. New York: HarperCollins, 1996.

Spong, John Shelby. *A New Christianity of a New World*. San Francisco: HarperCollins, 2001.

Teresa. *Mother Teresa: Come Be My Light—The Private Writings of the Saint of Calcutta*. New York: Doubleday Religion, 2007.

Wink, Walter. *Engaging the Powers*. Minneapolis: Fortress Press, 1992.

Winokur, Jon. *The Portable Curmudgeon*. New York: New American Library, 1987.

Inspiration

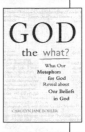

Finding Time for the Timeless: Spirituality in the Workweek
By John McQuiston II
Offers refreshing stories of everyday spiritual practices people use to free themselves from the work and worry mindset of our culture.
5⅛ x 6½, 208 pp, Quality PB, 978-1-59473-383-3 **$9.99**

God the *What*?: What Our Metaphors for God Reveal about Our Beliefs in God   *by Carolyn Jane Bohler*
Inspires you to consider a wide range of images of God in order to refine how you imagine God.   6 x 9, 192 pp, Quality PB, 978-1-59473-251-5 **$16.99**

How Did I Get to Be 70 When I'm 35 Inside?: Spiritual Surprises of Later Life   *by Linda Douty*
Encourages you to focus on the inner changes of aging to help you greet your later years as the grand adventure they can be.   6 x 9, 208 pp, Quality PB, 978-1-59473-297-3 **$16.99**

Restoring Life's Missing Pieces: The Spiritual Power of Remembering & Reuniting with People, Places, Things & Self   *by Caren Goldman*
A powerful and thought-provoking look at reunions of all kinds as roads to remembering and re membering ourselves.
6 x 9, 208 pp, Quality PB, 978-1-59473-295-9 **$16.99**

Saving Civility: 52 Ways to Tame Rude, Crude & Attitude for a Polite Planet
By Sara Hacala
Provides fifty-two practical ways you can reverse the course of incivility and make the world a more enriching, pleasant place to live.
6 x 9, 240 pp, Quality PB 978-1-59473-314-7 **$16.99**

Spiritually Healthy Divorce: Navigating Disruption with Insight & Hope
by Carolyne Call
A spiritual map to help you move through the twists and turns of divorce.
6 x 9, 224 pp, Quality PB, 978-1-59473-288-1 **$16.99**

Who Is My God? 2nd Edition
An Innovative Guide to Finding Your Spiritual Identity
by the Editors at SkyLight Paths
Provides the Spiritual Identity Self-Test™ to uncover the components of your unique spirituality.   6 x 9, 160 pp, Quality PB, 978-1-59473-014-6 **$15.99**

Journeys of Simplicity
Traveling Light with Thomas Merton, Bashō,
Edward Abbey, Annie Dillard & Others
by Philip Harnden
Invites you to consider a more graceful way of traveling through life.
PB includes journal pages to help you get started on
your own spiritual journey.
5 x 7¼, 144 pp, Quality PB, 978-1-59473-181-5 **$12.99**
5 x 7¼, 128 pp, HC, 978-1-893361-76-8 **$16.95**

Or phone, fax, mail or e-mail to: SKYLIGHT PATHS Publishing
Sunset Farm Offices, Route 4 • P.O. Box 237 • Woodstock, Vermont 05091
Tel: (802) 457-4000 • Fax: (802) 457-4004 • www.skylightpaths.com
Credit card orders: (800) 962-4544 (8:30AM–5:30PM EST Monday–Friday)
Generous discounts on quantity orders. SATISFACTION GUARANTEED. Prices subject to change.

Bible Stories / Folktales

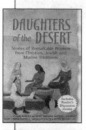

Abraham's Bind & Other Bible Tales of Trickery, Folly, Mercy and Love by Michael J. Caduto

New retellings of episodes in the lives of familiar biblical characters explore relevant life lessons. 6 x 9, 224 pp, HC, 978-1-59473-186-0 **$19.99**

Daughters of the Desert: Stories of Remarkable Women from Christian, Jewish and Muslim Traditions by Claire Rudolf Murphy,
Meghan Nuttall Sayres, Mary Cronk Farrell, Sarah Conover and Betsy Wharton

Breathes new life into the old tales of our female ancestors in faith. Uses traditional scriptural passages as starting points, then with vivid detail fills in historical context and place. Chapters reveal the voices of Sarah, Hagar, Huldah, Esther, Salome, Mary Magdalene, Lydia, Khadija, Fatima and many more. Historical fiction ideal for readers of all ages.

5½ x 8½, 192 pp, Quality PB, 978-1-59473-106-8 **$14.99** Inc. reader's discussion guide
HC, 978-1-893361-72-0 **$19.95**

The Triumph of Eve & Other Subversive Bible Tales
by Matt Biers-Ariel

These engaging retellings of familiar Bible stories are witty, often hilarious and always profound. They invite you to grapple with questions and issues that are often hidden in the original texts.

5½ x 8½, 192 pp, Quality PB, 978-1-59473-176-1 **$14.99**

Also available: The Triumph of Eve Teacher's Guide
8½ x 11, 44 pp, PB, 978-1-59473-152-5 **$8.99**

Wisdom in the Telling
Finding Inspiration and Grace in Traditional Folktales and Myths Retold
by Lorraine Hartin-Gelardi
6 x 9, 192 pp, HC, 978-1-59473-185-3 **$19.99**

Religious Etiquette / Reference

How to Be a Perfect Stranger, 5th Edition: The Essential Religious Etiquette Handbook Edited by Stuart M. Matlins and Arthur J. Magida

The indispensable guidebook to help the well-meaning guest when visiting other people's religious ceremonies. A straightforward guide to the rituals and celebrations of the major religions and denominations in the United States and Canada from the perspective of an interested guest of any other faith, based on information obtained from authorities of each religion. Belongs in every living room, library and office. Covers:

African American Methodist Churches • Assemblies of God • Bahá'í Faith • Baptist • Buddhist • Christian Church (Disciples of Christ) • Christian Science (Church of Christ, Scientist) • Churches of Christ • Episcopalian and Anglican • Hindu • Islam • Jehovah's Witnesses • Jewish • Lutheran • Mennonite/Amish • Methodist • Mormon (Church of Jesus Christ of Latter-day Saints) • Native American/First Nations • Orthodox Churches • Pentecostal Church of God • Presbyterian • Quaker (Religious Society of Friends) • Reformed Church in America/Canada • Roman Catholic • Seventh-day Adventist • Sikh • Unitarian Universalist • United Church of Canada • United Church of Christ

"The things Miss Manners forgot to tell us about religion."

—Los Angeles Times

"Finally, for those inclined to undertake their own spiritual journeys ... tells visitors what to expect." —New York Times

6 x 9, 432 pp, Quality PB, 978-1-59473-294-2 **$19.99**

The Perfect Stranger's Guide to Funerals and Grieving Practices: A Guide to Etiquette in Other People's Religious Ceremonies Edited by Stuart M. Matlins
6 x 9, 240 pp, Quality PB, 978-1-893361-20-1 **$16.95**

The Perfect Stranger's Guide to Wedding Ceremonies: A Guide to Etiquette in Other People's Religious Ceremonies Edited by Stuart M. Matlins
6 x 9, 208 pp, Quality PB, 978-1-893361-19-5 **$16.95**

Judaism / Christianity / Islam / Interfaith

All Politics Is Religious: Speaking Faith to the Media, Policy Makers and Community   *By Rabbi Dennis S. Ross; Foreword by Rev. Barry W. Lynn*
Provides ideas and strategies for expressing a clear, forceful and progressive religious point of view that is all too often overlooked and under-represented in public discourse.   6 x 9, 192 pp, Quality PB, 978-1-59473-374-1 **$18.99**

Religion Gone Astray: What We Found at the Heart of Interfaith
By Pastor Don Mackenzie, Rabbi Ted Falcon and Imam Jamal Rahman
Welcome to the deeper dimensions of interfaith dialogue—exploring that which divides us personally, spiritually and institutionally.
6 x 9, 192 pp, Quality PB, 978-1-59473-317-8 **$16.99**

Getting to the Heart of Interfaith: The Eye-Opening, Hope-Filled Friendship of a Pastor, a Rabbi & an Imam   *by Pastor Don Mackenzie, Rabbi Ted Falcon and Imam Jamal Rahman*
6 x 9, 192 pp, Quality PB, 978-1-59473-263-8 **$16.99**

Hearing the Call across Traditions: Readings on Faith and Service
Edited by Adam Davis; Foreword by Eboo Patel
6 x 9, 352 pp, Quality PB, 978-1-59473-303-1 **$18.99**; HC, 978-1-59473-264-5 **$29.99**

How to Do Good & Avoid Evil: A Global Ethic from the Sources of Judaism
by Hans Küng and Rabbi Walter Homolka; Translated by Rev. Dr. John Bowden
6 x 9, 224 pp, HC, 978-1-59473-255-3 **$19.99**

Blessed Relief: What Christians Can Learn from Buddhists about Suffering
by Gordon Peerman   6 x 9, 208 pp, Quality PB, 978-1-59473-252-2 **$16.99**

Christians & Jews—Faith to Faith: Tragic History, Promising Present, Fragile Future   *by Rabbi James Rudin*   6 x 9, 288 pp, HC, 978-1-58023-432-0 **$24.99***

Christians & Jews in Dialogue: Learning in the Presence of the Other   *by Mary C. Boys and Sara S. Lee; Foreword by Dorothy C. Bass*   6 x 9, 240 pp, Quality PB, 978-1-59473-254-6 **$18.99**

InterActive Faith: The Essential Interreligious Community-Building Handbook
Edited by Rev. Bud Heckman with Rori Picker Neiss; Foreword by Rev. Dirk Ficca
6 x 9, 304 pp, Quality PB, 978-1-59473-273-7 **$16.99**; HC, 978-1-59473-237-9 **$29.99**

The Jewish Approach to God: A Brief Introduction for Christians
by Rabbi Neil Gillman, PhD   5½ x 8½, 192 pp, Quality PB, 978-1-58023-190-9 **$16.95***

The Jewish Approach to Repairing the World (*Tikkun Olam*): A Brief Introduction for Christians   *by Rabbi Elliot N. Dorff, PhD, with Rev. Cory Willson*
5½ x 8½, 256 pp, Quality PB, 978-1-58023-349-1 **$16.99***

The Jewish Connection to Israel, the Promised Land: A Brief Introduction for Christians   *by Rabbi Eugene Korn, PhD*   5½ x 8½, 192 pp, Quality PB, 978-1-58023-318-7 **$14.99***

Jewish Holidays: A Brief Introduction for Christians   *by Rabbi Kerry M. Olitzky and Rabbi Daniel Judson*   5½ x 8½, 176 pp, Quality PB, 978-1-58023-302-6 **$16.99***

Jewish Ritual: A Brief Introduction for Christians
by Rabbi Kerry M. Olitzky and Rabbi Daniel Judson   5½ x 8½, 144 pp, Quality PB, 978-1-58023-210-4 **$14.99***

Jewish Spirituality: A Brief Introduction for Christians   *by Rabbi Lawrence Kushner*
5½ x 8½, 112 pp, Quality PB, 978-1-58023-150-3 **$12.95***

A Jewish Understanding of the New Testament   *by Rabbi Samuel Sandmel;*
New preface by Rabbi David Sandmel   5½ x 8½, 368 pp, Quality PB, 978-1-59473-048-1 **$19.99***

Modern Jews Engage the New Testament: Enhancing Jewish Well-Being in a Christian Environment   *by Rabbi Michael J. Cook, PhD*   6 x 9, 416 pp, HC, 978-1-58023-313-2 **$29.99***

Talking about God: Exploring the Meaning of Religious Life with Kierkegaard, Buber, Tillich and Heschel   *by Daniel F. Polish, PhD*   6 x 9, 160 pp, Quality PB, 978-1-59473-272-0 **$16.99**

We Jews and Jesus: Exploring Theological Differences for Mutual Understanding
by Rabbi Samuel Sandmel; New preface by Rabbi David Sandmel
6 x 9, 192 pp, Quality PB, 978-1-59473-208-9 **$16.99**

Who Are the *Real* Chosen People? The Meaning of Chosenness in Judaism, Christianity and Islam   *by Reuven Firestone, PhD*
6 x 9, 176 pp, Quality PB, 978-1-59473-290-4 **$16.99**; HC, 978-1-59473-248-5 **$21.99**

* A book from Jewish Lights, SkyLight Paths' sister imprint

Sacred Texts—SkyLight Illuminations Series

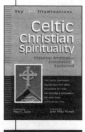

Offers today's spiritual seeker an enjoyable entry into the great classic texts of the world's spiritual traditions. Each classic is presented in an accessible translation, with facing pages of guided commentary from experts, giving you the keys you need to understand the history, context and meaning of the text.

CHRISTIANITY

Celtic Christian Spirituality: Essential Writings—Annotated & Explained
Annotation by Mary C. Earle; Foreword by John Philip Newell
Explores how the writings of this lively tradition embody the gospel.
5½ x 8½, 176 pp, Quality PB, 978-1-59473-302-4 **$16.99**

Desert Fathers and Mothers: Early Christian Wisdom Sayings—Annotated & Explained
Annotation by Christine Valters Paintner, PhD
Opens up wisdom of the desert fathers and mothers for readers with no previous knowledge of Western monasticism and early Christianity.
5½ x 8½, 192 pp, Quality PB, 978-1-59473-373-4 **$16.99**

The End of Days: Essential Selections from Apocalyptic Texts—Annotated & Explained
Annotation by Robert G. Clouse, PhD
Helps you understand the complex Christian visions of the end of the world.
5½ x 8½, 224 pp, Quality PB, 978-1-59473-170-9 **$16.99**

The Hidden Gospel of Matthew: Annotated & Explained
Translation & Annotation by Ron Miller
Discover the words and events that have the strongest connection to the historical Jesus.
5½ x 8½, 272 pp, Quality PB, 978-1-59473-038-2 **$16.99**

The Infancy Gospels of Jesus: Apocryphal Tales from the Childhoods of Mary and Jesus—Annotated & Explained
Translation & Annotation by Stevan Davies; Foreword by A. Edward Siecienski, PhD
A startling presentation of the early lives of Mary, Jesus and other biblical figures that will amuse and surprise you.
5½ x 8½, 176 pp, Quality PB, 978-1-59473-258-4 **$16.99**

John & Charles Wesley: Selections from Their Writings and Hymns—Annotated & Explained
Annotation by Paul W. Chilcote, PhD
A unique presentation of the writings of these two inspiring brothers brings together some of the most essential material from their large corpus of work.
5½ x 8½, 288 pp, Quality PB, 978-1-59473-309-3 **$16.99**

The Lost Sayings of Jesus: Teachings from Ancient Christian, Jewish, Gnostic and Islamic Sources—Annotated & Explained
Translation & Annotation by Andrew Phillip Smith; Foreword by Stephan A. Hoeller
This collection of more than three hundred sayings depicts Jesus as a Wisdom teacher who speaks to people of all faiths as a mystic and spiritual master.
5½ x 8½, 240 pp, Quality PB, 978-1-59473-172-3 **$16.99**

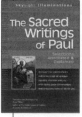

Philokalia: The Eastern Christian Spiritual Texts—Selections Annotated & Explained *Annotation by Allyne Smith; Translation by G. E. H. Palmer, Phillip Sherrard and Bishop Kallistos Ware*
The first approachable introduction to the wisdom of the Philokalia, the classic text of Eastern Christian spirituality.
5½ x 8½, 240 pp, Quality PB, 978-1-59473-103-7 **$16.99**

The Sacred Writings of Paul: Selections Annotated & Explained
Translation & Annotation by Ron Miller
Leads you into the exciting immediacy of Paul's teachings.
5½ x 8½, 224 pp, Quality PB, 978-1-59473-213-3 **$16.99**

Sacred Texts—continued

CHRISTIANITY—continued

Saint Augustine of Hippo: Selections from *Confessions* and Other Essential Writings—Annotated & Explained
Annotation by Joseph T. Kelley, PhD; Translation by the Augustinian Heritage Institute
Provides insight into the mind and heart of this foundational Christian figure.
5½ x 8½, 272 pp, Quality PB, 978-1-59473-282-9 **$16.99**

Saint Ignatius Loyola—The Spiritual Writings: Selections Annotated & Explained *Annotation by Mark Mossa, SJ*
Draws from contemporary translations of original texts focusing on the practical mysticism of Ignatius of Loyola.
5½ x 8½, 288 pp, Quality PB, 978-1-59473-301-7 **$16.99**

Sex Texts from the Bible: Selections Annotated & Explained
Translation & Annotation by Teresa J. Hornsby; Foreword by Amy-Jill Levine
Demystifies the Bible's ideas on gender roles, marriage, sexual orientation, virginity, lust and sexual pleasure.
5½ x 8½, 208 pp, Quality PB, 978-1-59473-217-1 **$16.99**

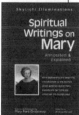

Spiritual Writings on Mary: Annotated & Explained
Annotation by Mary Ford-Grabowsky; Foreword by Andrew Harvey
Examines the role of Mary, the mother of Jesus, as a source of inspiration in history and in life today.
5½ x 8½, 288 pp, Quality PB, 978-1-59473-001-6 **$16.99**

The Way of a Pilgrim: The Jesus Prayer Journey—Annotated & Explained
Translation & Annotation by Gleb Pokrovsky; Foreword by Andrew Harvey
A classic of Russian Orthodox spirituality.
5½ x 8½, 160 pp, Illus., Quality PB, 978-1-893361-31-7 **$14.95**

GNOSTICISM

Gnostic Writings on the Soul: Annotated & Explained
Translation & Annotation by Andrew Phillip Smith; Foreword by Stephan A. Hoeller
Reveals the inspiring ways your soul can remember and return to its unique, divine purpose.
5½ x 8½, 144 pp, Quality PB, 978-1-59473-220-1 **$16.99**

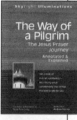

The Gospel of Philip: Annotated & Explained
Translation & Annotation by Andrew Phillip Smith; Foreword by Stevan Davies
Reveals otherwise unrecorded sayings of Jesus and fragments of Gnostic mythology.
5½ x 8½, 160 pp, Quality PB, 978-1-59473-111-2 **$16.99**

The Gospel of Thomas: Annotated & Explained
Translation & Annotation by Stevan Davies; Foreword by Andrew Harvey
Sheds new light on the origins of Christianity and portrays Jesus as a wisdom-loving sage.
5½ x 8½, 192 pp, Quality PB, 978-1-893361-45-4 **$16.99**

The Secret Book of John: The Gnostic Gospel—Annotated & Explained
Translation & Annotation by Stevan Davies
The most significant and influential text of the ancient Gnostic religion.
5½ x 8½, 208 pp, Quality PB, 978-1-59473-082-5 **$16.99**

Sacred Texts—continued

The Book of Job: Annotated & Explained
Translation and Annotation by Donald Kraus; Foreword by Dr. Marc Brettler
Clarifies for today's readers what Job is, how to overcome difficulties in the text, and what it may mean for us.
5½ x 8½, 256 pp, Quality PB, 978-1-59473-389-5 **$16.99**

The Divine Feminine in Biblical Wisdom Literature
Selections Annotated & Explained
Translation & Annotation by Rabbi Rami Shapiro; Foreword by Rev. Cynthia Bourgeault, PhD
Uses the Hebrew Bible and Wisdom literature to explain Sophia's way of wisdom and illustrate Her creative energy.
5½ x 8½, 240 pp, Quality PB, 978-1-59473-109-9 **$16.99**

Ecclesiastes: Annotated & Explained
Translation & Annotation by Rabbi Rami Shapiro; Foreword by Rev. Barbara Cawthorne Crafton
A timeless teaching on living well amid uncertainty and insecurity.
5½ x 8½, 160 pp, Quality PB, 978-1-59473-287-4 **$16.99**

Ethics of the Sages: *Pirke Avot*—Annotated & Explained
Translation & Annotation by Rabbi Rami Shapiro
Clarifies the ethical teachings of the early Rabbis.
5½ x 8½, 192 pp, Quality PB, 978-1-59473-207-2 **$16.99**

Hasidic Tales: Annotated & Explained
Translation & Annotation by Rabbi Rami Shapiro; Foreword by Andrew Harvey
Introduces the legendary tales of the impassioned Hasidic rabbis, presenting them as stories rather than as parables.
5½ x 8½, 240 pp, Quality PB, 978-1-893361-86-7 **$16.95**

The Hebrew Prophets: Selections Annotated & Explained
Translation & Annotation by Rabbi Rami Shapiro;
Foreword by Rabbi Zalman M. Schachter-Shalomi
5½ x 8½, 224 pp, Quality PB, 978-1-59473-037-5 **$16.99**

Maimonides—Essential Teachings on Jewish Faith & Ethics
The Book of Knowledge & the Thirteen Principles of Faith—Annotated & Explained
Translation and Annotation by Rabbi Marc D. Angel, PhD
Opens up for us Maimonides's views on the nature of God, providence, prophecy, free will, human nature, repentance and more.
5½ x 8½, 224 pp, Quality PB, 978-1-59473-311-6 **$18.99**

Proverbs: Annotated & Explained
Translation and Annotation by Rabbi Rami Shapiro
Demonstrates how these complex poetic forms are actually straightforward instructions to live simply, without rationalizations and excuses.
5½ x 8½, 288 pp, Quality PB, 978-1-59473-310-9 $16.99

***Tanya,* the Masterpiece of Hasidic Wisdom**
Selections Annotated & Explained
Translation & Annotation by Rabbi Rami Shapiro; Foreword by Rabbi Zalman M. Schachter-Shalomi
Clarifies one of the most powerful and potentially transformative books of Jewish wisdom.
5½ x 8½, 240 pp, Quality PB, 978-1-59473-275-1 **$16.99**

Zohar: Annotated & Explained
Translation & Annotation by Daniel C. Matt; Foreword by Andrew Harvey
The canonical text of Jewish mystical tradition.
5½ x 8½, 176 pp, Quality PB, 978-1-893361-51-5 **$16.99**

Spirituality

Gathering at God's Table: The Meaning of Mission in the Feast of Faith
By Katharine Jefferts Schori
A profound reminder of our role in the larger frame of God's dream for a restored and reconciled world. 6 x 9, 256 pp, HC, 978-1-59473-316-1 **$21.99**

The Heartbeat of God: Finding the Sacred in the Middle of Everything
by Katharine Jefferts Schori; Foreword by Joan Chittister, OSB
Explores our connections to other people, to other nations and with the environment through the lens of faith. 6 x 9, 240 pp, HC, 978-1-59473-292-8 **$21.99**

A Dangerous Dozen: Twelve Christians Who Threatened the Status Quo but Taught Us to Live Like Jesus
by the Rev. Canon C. K. Robertson, PhD; Foreword by Archbishop Desmond Tutu
Profiles twelve visionary men and women who challenged society and showed the world a different way of living. 6 x 9, 208 pp, Quality PB, 978-1-59473-298-0 **$16.99**

Decision Making & Spiritual Discernment: The Sacred Art of Finding Your Way *by Nancy L. Bieber*
Presents three essential aspects of Spirit-led decision making: willingness, attentiveness and responsiveness. 5½ x 8½, 208 pp, Quality PB, 978-1-59473-289-8 **$16.99**

Laugh Your Way to Grace: Reclaiming the Spiritual Power of Humor
by Rev. Susan Sparks A powerful, humorous case for laughter as a spiritual, healing path. 6 x 9, 176 pp, Quality PB, 978-1-59473-280-5 **$16.99**

Bread, Body, Spirit: Finding the Sacred in Food
Edited and with Introductions by Alice Peck 6 x 9, 224 pp, Quality PB, 978-1-59473-242-3 **$19.99**

Claiming Earth as Common Ground: The Ecological Crisis through the Lens of Faith
by Andrea Cohen-Kiener; Foreword by Rev. Sally Bingham
6 x 9, 192 pp, Quality PB, 978-1-59473-261-4 **$16.99**

Creating a Spiritual Retirement: A Guide to the Unseen Possibilities in Our Lives
by Molly Srode 6 x 9, 208 pp, b/w photos, Quality PB, 978-1-59473-050-4 **$14.99**

Creative Aging: Rethinking Retirement and Non-Retirement in a Changing World
by Marjory Zoet Bankson 6 x 9, 160 pp, Quality PB, 978-1-59473-281-2 **$16.99**

Keeping Spiritual Balance as We Grow Older: More than 65 Creative Ways to Use Purpose, Prayer, and the Power of Spirit to Build a Meaningful Retirement
by Molly and Bernie Srode 8 x 8, 224 pp, Quality PB, 978-1-59473-042-9 **$16.99**

Hearing the Call across Traditions: Readings on Faith and Service
Edited by Adam Davis; Foreword by Eboo Patel
6 x 9, 352 pp, Quality PB, 978-1-59473-303-1 **$18.99**; HC, 978-1-59473-264-5 **$29.99**

Honoring Motherhood: Prayers, Ceremonies & Blessings
Edited and with Introductions by Lynn L. Caruso
5 x 7¼, 272 pp, Quality PB, 978-1-58473-384-0 **$9.99**; HC, 978-1-59473-239-3 **$19.99**

The Losses of Our Lives: The Sacred Gifts of Renewal in Everyday Loss
by Dr. Nancy Copeland-Payton 6 x 9, 192 pp, HC, 978-1-59473-271-3 **$19.99**

Renewal in the Wilderness: A Spiritual Guide to Connecting with God in the Natural World *by John Lionberger*
6 x 9, 176 pp, b/w photos, Quality PB, 978-1-59473-219-5 **$16.99**

Soul Fire: Accessing Your Creativity
by Thomas Ryan, CSP 6 x 9, 160 pp, Quality PB, 978-1-59473-243-0 **$16.99**

A Spirituality for Brokenness: Discovering Your Deepest Self in Difficult Times
by Terry Taylor 6 x 9, 176 pp, Quality PB, 978-1-59473-229-4 **$16.99**

A Walk with Four Spiritual Guides: Krishna, Buddha, Jesus, and Ramakrishna
by Andrew Harvey 5½ x 8½, 192 pp, b/w photos & illus., Quality PB, 978-1-59473-138-9 **$15.99**

The Workplace and Spirituality: New Perspectives on Research and Practice
Edited by Dr. Joan Marques, Dr. Satinder Dhiman and Dr. Richard King
6 x 9, 256 pp, HC, 978-1-59473-260-7 **$29.99**

Children's Spirituality

Remembering My Grandparent: A Kid's Own Grief Workbook in the Christian Tradition *by Nechama Liss-Levinson, PhD, and Rev. Molly Phinney Baskette, MDiv* 8 x 10, 48 pp, 2-color text, HC, 978-1-59473-212-6 **$16.99** *For ages 7 & up*

Does God Ever Sleep? *by Joan Sauro, CSJ*
A charming nighttime reminder that God is always present in our lives.
10 x 8½, 32 pp, Full-color photos, Quality PB, 978-1-59473-110-5 **$8.99** *For ages 3–6*

Does God Forgive Me? *by August Gold; Full-color photos by Diane Hardy Waller*
Gently shows how God forgives all that we do if we are truly sorry.
10 x 8½, 32 pp, Full-color photos, Quality PB, 978-1-59473-142-6 **$8.99** *For ages 3–6*

God Said Amen *by Sandy Eisenberg Sasso; Full-color illus. by Avi Katz*
A warm and inspiring tale that shows us that we need only reach out to each other to find the answers to our prayers.
9 x 12, 32 pp, Full-color illus., HC, 978-1-58023-080-3 **$16.95*** *For ages 4 & up*

How Does God Listen? *by Kay Lindahl; Full-color photos by Cynthia Maloney*
How do we know when God is listening to us? Children will find the answers to these questions as they engage their senses while the story unfolds, learning how God listens in the wind, waves, clouds, hot chocolate, perfume, our tears and our laughter.
10 x 8½, 32 pp, Full-color photos, Quality PB, 978-1-59473-084-9 **$8.99** *For ages 3–6*

In God's Hands *by Lawrence Kushner and Gary Schmidt; Full-color illus. by Matthew J. Baek*
9 x 12, 32 pp, Full-color illus., HC, 978-1-58023-224-1 **$16.99*** *For ages 5 & up*

In God's Name *by Sandy Eisenberg Sasso; Full-color illus. by Phoebe Stone*
Like an ancient myth in its poetic text and vibrant illustrations, this award-winning modern fable about the search for God's name celebrates the diversity and, at the same time, the unity of all the people of the world.
9 x 12, 32 pp, Full-color illus., HC, 978-1-879045-26-2 **$16.99*** *For ages 4 & up*

Also available in Spanish: El nombre de Dios
9 x 12, 32 pp, Full-color illus., HC, 978-1-893361-63-8 **$16.95**

In Our Image: God's First Creatures
by Nancy Sohn Swartz; Full-color illus. by Melanie Hall
A playful new twist on the Genesis story—from the perspective of the animals. Celebrates the interconnectedness of nature and the harmony of all living things.
9 x 12, 32 pp, Full-color illus., HC, 978-1-879045-99-6 **$16.95*** *For ages 4 & up*

Noah's Wife: The Story of Naamah
by Sandy Eisenberg Sasso; Full-color illus. by Bethanne Andersen
Opens young readers' religious imaginations to new ideas about the well-known story of the Flood. When God tells Noah to bring the animals of the world onto the ark, God also calls on Naamah, Noah's wife, to save each plant on Earth.
9 x 12, 32 pp, Full-color illus., HC, 978-1-58023-134-3 **$16.95*** *For ages 4 & up*

Also available: Naamah: Noah's Wife (A Board Book)
by Sandy Eisenberg Sasso; Full-color illus. by Bethanne Andersen
5 x 5, 24 pp, Full-color illus., Board Book, 978-1-893361-56-0 **$7.95** *For ages 0–4*

Where Does God Live? *by August Gold and Matthew J. Perlman*
Helps children and their parents find God in the world around us with simple, practical examples children can relate to.
10 x 8½, 32 pp, Full-color photos, Quality PB, 978-1-893361-39-3 **$8.99** *For ages 3–6*

* A book from Jewish Lights, SkyLight Paths' sister imprint

Spiritual Practice

Fly-Fishing—The Sacred Art: Casting a Fly as a Spiritual Practice
by Rabbi Eric Eisenkramer and Rev. Michael Attas, MD; Foreword by Chris Wood, CEO,
Trout Unlimited; Preface by Lori Simon, executive director, Casting for Recovery
Shares what fly-fishing can teach you about reflection, awe and wonder; the benefits of solitude; the blessing of community and the search for the Divine.
5½ x 8½, 160 pp, Quality PB, 978-1-59473-299-7 **$16.99**

Lectio Divina—The Sacred Art: Transforming Words & Images into Heart-Centered Prayer *by Christine Valters Paintner, PhD*
Expands the practice of sacred reading beyond scriptural texts and makes it accessible in contemporary life. 5½ x 8½, 240 pp, Quality PB, 978-1-59473-300-0 **$16.99**

Writing—The Sacred Art: Beyond the Page to Spiritual Practice
By Rami Shapiro and Aaron Shapiro
Push your writing through the trite and the boring to something fresh, something transformative. Includes over fifty unique, practical exercises.
5½ x 8½, 192 pp, Quality PB, 978-1-59473-372-7 **$16.99**

Dance—The Sacred Art: The Joy of Movement as a Spiritual Practice
by Cynthia Winton-Henry 5½ x 8½, 224 pp, Quality PB, 978-1-59473-268-3 **$16.99**

Everyday Herbs in Spiritual Life: A Guide to Many Practices
by Michael J. Caduto; Foreword by Rosemary Gladstar
7 x 9, 208 pp, 20+ b/w illus., Quality PB, 978-1-59473-174-7 **$16.99**

Giving—The Sacred Art: Creating a Lifestyle of Generosity
by Lauren Tyler Wright 5½ x 8½, 208 pp, Quality PB, 978-1-59473-224-9 **$16.99**

Haiku—The Sacred Art: A Spiritual Practice in Three Lines
by Margaret D. McGee 5½ x 8½, 192 pp, Quality PB, 978-1-59473-269-0 **$16.99**

Hospitality—The Sacred Art: Discovering the Hidden Spiritual Power of Invitation and Welcome *by Rev. Nanette Sawyer; Foreword by Rev. Dirk Ficca*
5½ x 8½, 208 pp, Quality PB, 978-1-59473-228-7 **$16.99**

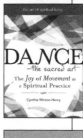

Labyrinths from the Outside In: Walking to Spiritual Insight—A Beginner's Guide
by Donna Schaper and Carole Ann Camp
6 x 9, 208 pp, b/w illus. and photos, Quality PB, 978-1-893361-18-8 **$16.95**

Practicing the Sacred Art of Listening: A Guide to Enrich Your Relationships
and Kindle Your Spiritual Life *by Kay Lindahl* 8 x 8, 176 pp, Quality PB, 978-1-893361-85-0 **$16.95**

Recovery—The Sacred Art: The Twelve Steps as Spiritual Practice *by Rami Shapiro;*
Foreword by Joan Borysenko, PhD 5½ x 8½, 240 pp, Quality PB, 978-1-59473-259-1 **$16.99**

Running—The Sacred Art: Preparing to Practice *by Dr. Warren A. Kay; Foreword by*
Kristin Armstrong 5½ x 8½, 160 pp, Quality PB, 978-1-59473-227-0 **$16.99**

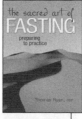

The Sacred Art of Chant: Preparing to Practice
by Ana Hernández 5½ x 8½, 192 pp, Quality PB, 978-1-59473-036-8 **$16.99**

The Sacred Art of Fasting: Preparing to Practice
by Thomas Ryan, CSP 5½ x 8½, 192 pp, Quality PB, 978-1-59473-078-8 **$15.99**

The Sacred Art of Forgiveness: Forgiving Ourselves and Others through God's
Grace *by Marcia Ford* 8 x 8, 176 pp, Quality PB, 978-1-59473-175-4 **$18.99**

The Sacred Art of Listening: Forty Reflections for Cultivating a Spiritual Practice
by Kay Lindahl; Illus. by Amy Schnapper 8 x 8, 160 pp, b/w illus., Quality PB, 978-1-893361-44-7 **$16.99**

The Sacred Art of Lovingkindness: Preparing to Practice
by Rabbi Rami Shapiro; Foreword by Marcia Ford 5½ x 8½, 176 pp, Quality PB, 978-1-59473-151-8 **$16.99**

Sacred Attention: A Spiritual Practice for Finding God in the Moment
by Margaret D. McGee 6 x 9, 144 pp, Quality PB, 978-1-59473-291-1 **$16.99**

Soul Fire: Accessing Your Creativity
by Thomas Ryan, CSP 6 x 9, 160 pp, Quality PB, 978-1-59473-243-0 **$16.99**

Spiritual Adventures in the Snow: Skiing & Snowboarding as Renewal for Your Soul
by Dr. Marcia McFee and Rev. Karen Foster; Foreword by Paul Arthur
5½ x 8½, 208 pp, Quality PB, 978-1-59473-270-6 **$16.99**

Thanking & Blessing—The Sacred Art: Spiritual Vitality through Gratefulness
by Jay Marshall, PhD; Foreword by Philip Gulley 5½ x 8½, 176 pp, Quality PB, 978-1-59473-231-7 **$16.99**

Prayer / Meditation

Men Pray: Voices of Strength, Faith, Healing, Hope and Courage
Created by the Editors at SkyLight Paths
Celebrates the rich variety of ways men around the world have called out to the
Divine—with words of joy, praise, gratitude, wonder, petition and even anger—
from the ancient world up to our own day.
5 x 7¼, 192 pp, HC, 978-1-59473-395-6 **$16.99**

Sacred Attention: A Spiritual Practice for Finding God in the Moment
by Margaret D. McGee
Framed on the Christian liturgical year, this inspiring guide explores ways to
develop a practice of attention as a means of talking—and listening—to God.
6 x 9, 144 pp, Quality PB, 978-1-59473-291-1 **$16.99**

Women of Color Pray: Voices of Strength, Faith, Healing, Hope and Courage
Edited and with Introductions by Christal M. Jackson
Through these prayers, poetry, lyrics, meditations and affirmations, you will share
in the strong and undeniable connection women of color share with God.
5 x 7¼, 208 pp, Quality PB, 978-1-59473-077-1 **$15.99**

The Art of Public Prayer, 2nd Edition: Not for Clergy Only
by Lawrence A. Hoffman, PhD 6 x 9, 288 pp, Quality PB, 978-1-893361-06-5 **$19.99**

A Heart of Stillness: A Complete Guide to Learning the Art of Meditation
by David A. Cooper 5½ x 8½, 272 pp, Quality PB, 978-1-893361-03-4 **$18.99**

Living into Hope: A Call to Spiritual Action for Such a Time as This
by Rev. Dr. Joan Brown Campbell; Foreword by Karen Armstrong
6 x 9, 208 pp, HC, 978-1-59473-283-6 **$21.99**

Meditation without Gurus: A Guide to the Heart of Practice
by Clark Strand 5½ x 8½, 192 pp, Quality PB, 978-1-893361-93-5 **$16.95**

Prayers to an Evolutionary God
by William Cleary; Afterword by Diarmuid O'Murchu
6 x 9, 208 pp, HC, 978-1-59473-006-1 **$21.99**

Praying with Our Hands: 21 Practices of Embodied Prayer from the World's
Spiritual Traditions *by Jon M. Sweeney; Photos by Jennifer J. Wilson; Foreword by Mother Tessa
Bielecki; Afterword by Taitetsu Unno, PhD*
8 x 8, 96 pp, 22 duotone photos, Quality PB, 978-1-893361-16-4 **$16.95**

Secrets of Prayer: A Multifaith Guide to Creating Personal Prayer in Your Life
by Nancy Corcoran, CSJ
6 x 9, 160 pp, Quality PB, 978-1-59473-215-7 **$16.99**

Three Gates to Meditation Practice: A Personal Journey into Sufism, Buddhism,
and Judaism *by David A. Cooper* 5½ x 8½, 240 pp, Quality PB, 978-1-893361-22-5 **$16.95**

Prayer / M. Basil Pennington, OCSO

Finding Grace at the Center, 3rd Edition: The Beginning of
Centering Prayer *with Thomas Keating, OCSO, and Thomas E. Clarke, SJ; Foreword by Rev.
Cynthia Bourgeault, PhD* A practical guide to a simple and beautiful form of medita-
tive prayer. 5 x 7¼, 128 pp, Quality PB, 978-1-59473-182-2 **$12.99**

The Monks of Mount Athos: A Western Monk's Extraordinary
Spiritual Journey on Eastern Holy Ground *Foreword by Archimandrite Dionysios*
Explores the landscape, monastic communities and food of Athos.
6 x 9, 352 pp, Quality PB, 978-1-893361-78-2 **$18.95**

Psalms: A Spiritual Commentary *Illus. by Phillip Ratner*
Reflections on some of the most beloved passages from the Bible's most widely
read book. 6 x 9, 176 pp, 24 full-page b/w illus., Quality PB, 978-1-59473-234-8 **$16.99**

The Song of Songs: A Spiritual Commentary *Illus. by Phillip Ratner*
Explore the Bible's most challenging mystical text.
6 x 9, 160 pp, 14 full-page b/w illus., Quality PB, 978-1-59473-235-5 **$16.99**
HC, 978-1-59473-004-7 **$19.99**

Women's Interest

Women, Spirituality and Transformative Leadership
Where Grace Meets Power
Edited by Kathe Schaaf, Kay Lindahl, Kathleen S. Hurty, PhD, and Reverend Guo Cheen
A dynamic conversation on the power of women's spiritual leadership and its emerging patterns of transformation. 6 x 9, 288 pp, Hardcover, 978-1-59473-313-0 **$24.99**

Spiritually Healthy Divorce: Navigating Disruption with Insight & Hope
by Carolyne Call A spiritual map to help you move through the twists and turns of divorce. 6 x 9, 224 pp, Quality PB, 978-1-59473-288-1 **$16.99**

New Feminist Christianity: Many Voices, Many Views
Edited by Mary E. Hunt and Diann L. Neu
Insights from ministers and theologians, activists and leaders, artists and liturgists who are shaping the future. Taken together, their voices offer a starting point for building new models of religious life and worship.
6 x 9, 384 pp, HC, 978-1-59473-285-0 **$24.99**

New Jewish Feminism: Probing the Past, Forging the Future
Edited by Rabbi Elyse Goldstein; Foreword by Anita Diamant
Looks at the growth and accomplishments of Jewish feminism and what they mean for Jewish women today and tomorrow. Features the voices of women from every area of Jewish life, addressing the important issues that concern Jewish women.
6 x 9, 480 pp, Quality PB, 978-1-58023-448-1 **$19.99**; HC, 978-1-58023-359-0 **$24.99***

Bread, Body, Spirit: Finding the Sacred in Food
Edited and with Introductions by Alice Peck 6 x 9, 224 pp, Quality PB, 978-1-59473-242-3 **$19.99**

Dance—The Sacred Art: The Joy of Movement as a Spiritual Practice
by Cynthia Winton-Henry 5½ x 8½, 224 pp, Quality PB, 978-1-59473-268-3 **$16.99**

Daughters of the Desert: Stories of Remarkable Women from Christian, Jewish and Muslim Traditions
by Claire Rudolf Murphy, Meghan Nuttall Sayres, Mary Cronk Farrell, Sarah Conover and Betsy Wharton
5½ x 8½, 192 pp, Illus., Quality PB, 978-1-59473-106-8 **$14.99** Inc. reader's discussion guide

The Divine Feminine in Biblical Wisdom Literature
Selections Annotated & Explained
Translation & Annotation by Rabbi Rami Shapiro; Foreword by Rev. Cynthia Bourgeault, PhD
5½ x 8½, 240 pp, Quality PB, 978-1-59473-109-9 **$16.99**

Divining the Body: Reclaim the Holiness of Your Physical Self
by Jan Phillips 8 x 8, 256 pp, Quality PB, 978-1-59473-080-1 **$18.99**

Honoring Motherhood: Prayers, Ceremonies & Blessings
Edited and with Introductions by Lynn L. Caruso
5 x 7¼, 272 pp, Quality PB, 978-1-58473-384-0 **$9.99**; HC, 978-1-59473-239-3 **$19.99**

Next to Godliness: Finding the Sacred in Housekeeping
Edited by Alice Peck 6 x 9, 224 pp, Quality PB, 978-1-59473-214-0 **$19.99**

ReVisions: Seeing Torah through a Feminist Lens
by Rabbi Elyse Goldstein 5½ x 8½, 224 pp, Quality PB, 978-1-58023-117-6 **$16.95***

The Triumph of Eve & Other Subversive Bible Tales
by Matt Biers-Ariel 5½ x 8½, 192 pp, Quality PB, 978-1-59473-176-1 **$14.99**

White Fire: A Portrait of Women Spiritual Leaders in America
by Malka Drucker; Photos by Gay Block 7 x 10, 320 pp, b/w photos, HC, 978-1-893361-64-5 **$24.95**

Woman Spirit Awakening in Nature: Growing Into the Fullness of Who You Are
by Nancy Barrett Chickerneo, PhD; Foreword by Eileen Fisher
8 x 8, 224 pp, b/w illus., Quality PB, 978-1-59473-250-8 **$16.99**

Women of Color Pray: Voices of Strength, Faith, Healing, Hope and Courage
Edited and with Introductions by Christal M. Jackson
5 x 7¼, 208 pp, Quality PB, 978-1-59473-077-1 **$15.99**

The Women's Torah Commentary: New Insights from Women Rabbis on the 54 Weekly Torah Portions *Edited by Rabbi Elyse Goldstein*
6 x 9, 496 pp, Quality PB, 978-1-58023-370-5 **$19.99**; HC, 978-1-58023-076-6 **$34.95***

* A book from Jewish Lights, SkyLight Paths' sister imprint

About SKYLIGHT PATHS Publishing

SkyLight Paths Publishing is creating a place where people of different spiritual traditions come together for challenge and inspiration, a place where we can help each other understand the mystery that lies at the heart of our existence.

Through spirituality, our religious beliefs are increasingly becoming a part of our lives—rather than *apart* from our lives. While many of us may be more interested than ever in spiritual growth, we may be less firmly planted in traditional religion. Yet, we do want to deepen our relationship to the sacred, to learn from our own as well as from other faith traditions, and to practice in new ways.

SkyLight Paths sees both believers and seekers as a community that increasingly transcends traditional boundaries of religion and denomination—people wanting to learn from each other, *walking together, finding the way*.

For your information and convenience, at the back of this book we have provided a list of other SkyLight Paths books you might find interesting and useful. They cover the following subjects:

Buddhism / Zen	Global Spiritual	Monasticism
Catholicism	Perspectives	Mysticism
Children's Books	Gnosticism	Poetry
Christianity	Hinduism /	Prayer
Comparative	Vedanta	Religious Etiquette
Religion	Inspiration	Retirement
Current Events	Islam / Sufism	Spiritual Biography
Earth-Based	Judaism	Spiritual Direction
Spirituality	Kabbalah	Spirituality
Enneagram	Meditation	Women's Interest
	Midrash Fiction	Worship

Or phone, fax, mail or e-mail to: SKYLIGHT PATHS Publishing
Sunset Farm Offices, Route 4 • P.O. Box 237 • Woodstock, Vermont 05091
Tel: (802) 457-4000 • Fax: (802) 457-4004 • www.skylightpaths.com
Credit card orders: (800) 962-4544 (8:30AM–5:30PM EST Monday–Friday)
Generous discounts on quantity orders. SATISFACTION GUARANTEED. Prices subject to change.